BREAKING
RANKS

www.wilkinsonpublishing.com.au

Published by:
Wilkinson Publishing Pty Ltd
ACN 006 042 173
PO Box 24135, Melbourne, Victoria, Australia, 3001
Ph: +61 3 9654 5446
www.wilkinsonpublishing.com.au

Cover art Lee Walker based on a concept by Jess Lomas.
Internal design Lee Walker.

 A catalogue record for this book is available from the National Library of Australia

Planned date of publication: February 2021
Title: Breaking Ranks
ISBN(s): 9781925927481 Printed - Paperback.
Printed and bound in Australia by Griffin Press, part of Ovato

BREAKING RANKS

JOE NOONAN

INTRODUCTION

The 1980s in Victoria was a hard time to be on either side of the law. There was a war raging between crooks and coppers that left a death toll that resulted in a Coronial Enquiry into police shootings.

This was for all intents and purposes a civil war for the right to control the state. Who won and who lost is hard to say? Both sides took heavy casualties and sometimes the lines were blurred between right and wrong. Most of those crooks are dead now. Most of those coppers are alive. Numerically at least you'd have to notch up the victory to the coppers.

The crooks were deadly serious and were carrying out regular armed robberies on banks and armoured cash transport vehicles. They were armed with weapons of all descriptions from pistols, revolvers, shotguns, sawn off rifles and some military-style weapons. They had no dramas firing shots during their stick ups and thought nothing of the physical and mental scars they branded bank staff and customers with during their rampage.

The Victoria Police Armed Robbery Squad played a major part in the war against these highly organised and desperate gangs. The fight was waged over six or seven years with the whole state, and indeed the country kept informed blow by blow in the press. The Major Crime Squad was another tough branch of the Criminal Investigation Branch more commonly known as the CIB.

The Majors and the Robbers were on the same floor at the St Kilda Road Police Complex and often assisted each other on jobs. I was a Detective Senior Constable, more commonly referred to as a Senior Detective, attached to the Majors and just happened to be at the right spot at the wrong time more often than not. Or was it the other way round? I bore witness to and was engaged in some of the enquiries and aftermaths of several shootings and murders, beatings and a variety of police stories from my time in the Victoria Police.

These days everyone drops all the shootings and deaths under the Underbelly umbrella. I don't know how they got that tag, but it stuck and has been dramatised and to a degree popularised in recent years. They described the war mainly between the crooks and rival gangs, which involved the police but wasn't centred around them. There were some coppers that allegedly aligned themselves with different sides in this war but weren't on the front line.

The 1980s was the scene of a different war. It wasn't crook against crook. It was crooks against coppers. The stakes were high. The control of law and order in Victoria.

That six- or seven-year period saw more shootings deaths of crooks in Victoria than the rest of the country combined. Considering the size and population of Victoria, it was considered we were punching well above our weight.

I am pretty sure we had more police shootings in those days than the New York Police Department. It was on for young and old and at times resembled the Wild West. There were shoot outs in shopping centres and other public places that involved Victorians going about their daily lives. It was this aspect of the war that made it personal, not only to coppers and crooks, but the average Victorian. This public face got everyone involved and the papers and media in general had a field day.

My life before and after Walsh Street was never dull. Like most people, I enjoyed numerous highs and several lows but overall have lived a full and thoroughly enjoyable life. My police career finished with Walsh Street.

CHAPTER ONE

The Walsh Street Police Murders

On 12 October 1988, my life was to take a new direction by a unique mix of cowardice and bastardry in the form of the murder of Constables Steven Tynan and Damien Eyre in Walsh Street, South Yarra. It was the battle that would prove pivotal and ultimately decide the war between the coppers and the crooks.

Constables Tynan and Eyre were shot to death by a gang of gutless crooks at about 4.47am on that fateful day. Their murders sparked what would become the largest police investigation in Victoria — and Australia — at that time.

I was working at the Major Crime Squad and we were starting early that morning to do a raid on a suspect. I'd just picked up one of the other blokes from the Majors from his unit in a suburb just outside the CBD.

We were heading to our office in St Kilda Road just after 5am. We had the police radio in the unmarked CIB car and we came up on the air to say we were on duty. The operator asked us to contact D24 by phone urgently. I looked at my passenger and we had no idea what the hell was going on.

As we didn't have mobile phones in those days, I pulled over and called D24 from a telephone box. I was put through to the operator and gave him our call sign, which was Crime 550. He asked what squad we were from and I told him the Major Crime Squad.

He told me that two uniform members had been shot in Walsh Street South Yarra and that it didn't look good. He told me to head to that location and take direction from the Homicide Squad, who were on their way to take control of the scene.

When the operator told me the news, the hair stood up on the back of my neck and I felt physically ill.

I immediately flashed back to the scene of Constable Neil Clinch's shooting the previous year and I momentarily returned there and relived my mental pictures of him lying critically wounded in uniform.

I got back in the car and we sped all the way to the scene of the shootings in Walsh Street. I don't remember what, if anything, we talked about on the way, I was more concentrating on getting there than talking. Luckily the traffic was very light at that time of the morning and we made extremely good time.

I remember pulling up near the scene, but it was from a distance and I had nothing to do with the initial crime scene processing. We would take witness statements during the processing of the scene some hours later but at the initial time of arrival we stayed out and looked on. It was like watching something out of a movie.

Even though we were well away, I could see the stolen car with the driver's door open, the blood stains and the medical waste left by the attending ambulance crews. This again made me think of the Neil Clinch scene, as there were trademark signs when seriously wounded people are treated.

The transcript of the D24 Communications recording is chilling and puts you in scene for what happened that morning. Think of yourself driving around the Melbourne area that morning within a couple of hours of knocking off and hearing this come over the radio in your police car. Imagine looking at the person you're working with and trying to comprehend what the hell was happening.

At about 4.38am that morning, the D24 radio operator Sgt Beaton had given the job to Prahran 311 to check out a suspect vehicle in Walsh Street South Yarra. They had acknowledged and headed to the location. The call sign of Prahran 311 meant it was the divvy van working from 11pm to 7am from Prahran Police Station.

At 4.51 Sgt Beaton tried to raise the van crew of Tynan and Eyre and not being able to, the following transcript gives an eerie insight into what happened.

D24: VKC to Prahran 311. (Pause). VKC to Prahran 311. (Pause). VKC to South Melbourne 250, any unit clear near Walsh Street South Yarra. (Pause) VKC to Prahran 311, South Melbourne 250, any unit clear near Walsh Street, South Yarra.

The call is getting escalated and when it got to 'any unit clear'. It normally meant the job was serious and had to be attended quickly rather than left to wait until someone was clear. The voices on the tape become more excited and to anyone who has heard that tape makes the hair on your neck stand up.

ASM150: South Melbourne 150. *(The duty inspector using a portable radio from within the South Melbourne Police Station.)*
D24: South Melbourne 150.
ASM150: South 150, I'm in the area near South Yarra.
D24: South Melbourne 150. I sent Prahran 311 down to Walsh Street. There's a car, a white Holden sedan parked in the middle of the road with lights on and smashed windows. Since then I've had about three or four cards *(Each card contained details of caller and the job and was sent via a conveyor to the operator)* come down saying that they've heard shots fired in that street and I can't get Prahran 311 at this stage.

This last message has just escalated the job to the most urgent possible. Shots fired and attending police have not responded to radio summons. No-one working that morning would have contemplated what was to come. They would have been scrambling from whatever they were doing to respond to this call. The heart would be pumping, the hair on the back of the neck would be at attention and there would be a queasy feeling in the pit of the stomach.

ASM150: South Melbourne 150. On my way.

D24: Roger. Is there any other unit?

ARS621: Russell Street 621, we can head that way.

D24: 621 roger.

ISK311: St Kilda 311. Do you want us to go down?

D24: Affirmative.

ARS650: 650. Would you like us to assist?

D24: 650. If you want.

ARS650: Unintelligible

D24: Unit calling?

ARS650: 650. What was the location of the last?

D24: Walsh Street South Yarra.

ARS650: Roger that.

ASM250: South Melbourne 250. We're clear of South heading to that one in Prahran. *(The call sign 250 meant there was a sergeant on board from South Melbourne.)*

D24: Roger. And the first unit down there give us a sit rep thanks and take care. I sent Prahran 311 down there and haven't heard from him since. South Melbourne 250. There's one complainant a Mrs Borg from Walsh Street says she heard approximately three of four shots. She saw a male run into a lane behind the flats there and into Airlie Street and then into Punt Road. She also saw a white car in the street and another man chasing after him.

Even just typing this I experience what every other copper in the world would feel on hearing this last report from D24. Shots fired have been confirmed and the police are not accounted for. Although probably thinking the worst the other police en route couldn't comprehend the scene. I have seen it far too many times and I still can't believe it. The responding police would be in full emergency approach and driving like bats out of buggery to get there as soon as possible.

D24: Russell Street 650.
ARS650: 650.
D24: Can you come down Punt Road and have a look around there?
ARS650: 650. Roger that.

Now realising there is a chance shots have been fired and people seen running all over the joint, the operator would start to think about spreading out the response to try and cover as many locations mentioned as possible. That way if it was police chasing the crooks they would get help sooner. If it was just the crooks, hopefully that could be caught on the hop.

The D24 office would have had additional police responding to assist Sergeant Beaton and would be bringing up maps of the area on the console computer to start grid coverage of the area. No doubt the senior police member at D24 would have been alerted and would be live monitoring the calls. The procedures would be checked for police shooting response and everyone at D24 would be well and truly awake and firing on all cylinders, whilst still hoping for the best for the two young policemen.

ISK350: St Kilda 350. (*This would signify a sergeant has come out in another van apart from the usual 311 divvy van to respond.*)
D24: St Kilda 350.

ISK350: On route to your last. What's the address again thanks?

D24: It's 220 Walsh Street in South Yarra and the last we've heard was a person running up into Punt Road with another man chasing after him.

ASM250: South 250, urgent. South 250 urgent.

D24: Unit calling?

ASM250: South Melbourne 250. Two members down. Urgent.

Just typing these words and remembering listening to the voices of these people during this most terrible of scenes makes me get cold chills all over. Now there was no doubt. Two police had been shot. The world had changed for everyone. Everyone at the scene were on virgin ground as far as training went. There was no policy or procedure for this type of outrage. This was inconceivable.

D24: Roger. Need an ambulance?

ASM250: 250 urgent. Yes an ambulance please. Two members down.

ACW250: City West 250 do you need any assistance?

D24: City West 250 affirmative.

ASM250: South Melbourne 250, for God's sake get an ambulance.

D24: Yeah we're getting one now.

ASM250: South Melbourne 250 we need an ambulance. We've got two members down with gunshot wounds outside 222 Walsh Street, 222 Walsh Street.

D24: All members take care.

ASM250: Unintelligible

D24: Unit Calling?

ASM250: South Melbourne250. Hurry up. We'll need a MICA ambulance for these two…

A MICA ambulance was a Mobile Intensive Care Ambulance which was referred only when attending police knew there was more help needed that a normal ambulance could provide. The sergeant from South Melbourne had seen the injuries and knew these two young blokes needed everything available if they had any chance.

The crooks had set up a stolen Commodore Sedan in the middle of Walsh Street and then someone had called D24 and made the report of a stolen car at that location. As the transcript details, the Prahran divisional van got the job and made their way to the car. What happened next was one of the most cowardly and despicable acts of violence ever perpetrated in Victorian policing history.

As Constables Tynan and Eyre pulled up behind the suspect vehicle, they performed a cursory inspection of what would have appeared a most innocuous job. How many vans before and after this had attended a stolen and abandoned car left in a quiet street? I can only imagine that nothing sinister would have crossed the minds of these two young coppers when they took the job.

The time was of significance as well. On night shift the worst time is between 4 and 5am. I used to feel like death warmed up. The thrill of the busy times were over and I couldn't wait to hit 7am and knock off. The senses were not at their best around the bewitching hour and I have no doubt these young blokes would have been feeling the effects of the time.

What happened next has been recreated by forensic experts and is summarised as this. Steven Tynan had gone to the driver's door and sat in the seat and was looking inside the suspect car. Damian Eyre was standing outside the driver's door looking in. Tynan was hit by a shotgun blast just as he was going to get out of the car. The force of the blast pushed him back into the car and caused massive head injuries.

Eyre was shot across the back and shoulder as he squatted next to Tynan in the open doorway of the car. No doubt he would be reacting to the first shot when he was wounded. Damian Eyre somehow managed to get up and wrestle with one of the gutless bastards who had ambushed them. Another shot was fired and hit a wall nearby.

Then during the struggle, another crook has intervened and taken Eyre's firearm from his holster whilst he was fighting the first crook. The second crook then shot him point blank in the head and he fell to the road near the rear driver's side wheel. The mongrel bastard then shot him in the back again using the police issued 38 revolver. These cowardly bastards relied on numbers and ambush to get the upper hand and enable them to do what they did.

This was the scene confronting the attending police. It is something no one involved will ever forget or get over. Heaven and the Police Honour Roll had two new members.

Hell will still be waiting for those gutless cowards not already dead as I write this.

We eventually headed back to our office in St Kilda Road and waited for the hierarchy, who planned the response to the murders. We ended up going to Walsh Street a couple of hours after the murders to assist taking statements from some of the tenants of the many houses and units in and around the scene of the shootings.

For the next week the Armed Robbery Squad and the Major Crime Squad were used to do some heavy raids on well-known crooks, illegal gaming houses and anywhere else that pressure could be applied, to try and gather any intelligence.

We crashed in doors on houses, flats, businesses and pubs where crooks lived, worked or frequented.

We spoke to members of the so-called underworld who were shocked at the brazen slayings. I'm not for one minute saying that some of these crooks gave a rat's arse about coppers being killed. From their point of view, it was bad business and they understood our response and level of activity would be maintained, until we found out something to help us.

Every illegal card game was closed down until further notice. It was an eye opener going to these places with my boss Peter Spence and I never ceased to be amazed at his ability to garner information or intelligence from them. He was a hard man and some of these blokes were hard men too. I think there existed some form of mutual respect, even if they came from different sides of the tracks.

Either that or the boss did a very good job of intimidating them, so that they appeared friendly, when in fact it may have been fear that motivated their assistance. Either way the crooks were staying tight as your auntie's tracksuit pants. No one was giving the coppers an inch.

Crooks were staying home as some feared they might become reprisal targets for a very angry police force. As it turned out that probably wasn't a bad idea.

The circumstances of the Graeme Jensen shooting on the 11th of October by the Armed Robbery Squad were foremost in every good crook's mind. Many believed that shooting was suspect and that he'd been shot and fitted up with a firearm after his death.

It was the precursor of disaster to come, being the murders of Tynan and Eyre the next day. It resulted in eight Armed Robbery Squad detectives and one Homicide Squad detective being charged with the wilful murder of Graeme Jensen. Seven had their charges dropped, as it was deemed that there was insufficient evidence to take them to trial. The remaining detective went to trial and was acquitted.

Jensen's shooting was the advent of change for many police and many crooks.

His shooting came close on the heels of two other shootings involving the Armed Robbery Squad, the deaths of Mark Militano and Frank Valastro, which were also spoken about by crooks as further instances of suspect police shootings.

No one was ever charged or faced trial over those deaths and the allegations by other crooks that they were 'taken out' is wholly supposition on their part.

The Walsh Street Task Force was my first glimpse of task force policing and I didn't really understand the intricacies in setting one up properly and the importance of managing it.

As it would pan out, I obviously wasn't alone. The Walsh Street or Tynan-Eyre Task Force was the team tasked with the investigation and prosecution of the bastards responsible.

We were all committed to a common purpose and it is this common purpose that many in the corporate world will never fully understand. The closeness enjoyed by police and emergency service workers, and from what I am told, the military, isn't easily described. I think it stems from working on some tasks that most people would never do, in tragic and sometimes life-threatening circumstances that weld individuals together. That relationship is formed when people rely on each other for their continued existence and welfare.

CHAPTER TWO

The Task Force is Born

On 24 October 1988, some 12 days after the murders, it was announced that a task force would finally be established to investigate.

Apparently the creation of the task force had been opposed by some senior police, as they believed they'd lose control of the investigation if the team left the Homicide Squad's office.

Part of me wanted to be on that investigation team. Another part was unsure as to what effect it would have on those tasked with the holy grail of policing — tracking down offenders for the brutal murder of two policemen.

There was no greater challenge and as I was to discover the road wasn't going to be an easy one to travel and the impact it'd have on the rest of my life would be considerable. The Tye-Eyre Task Force was born and any concept of normality was killed as a result.

The Task Force Investigation Team was to be headed by a Detective Chief Inspector seconded from the Homicide Squad. There were two Detective Inspectors — Dave Sprague and my elder brother, John Noonan, both of the Homicide Squad.

The rest of the Task Force was seconded mainly from the Armed Robbery, Major Crime and Homicide Squads, with a few regional CIB Detectives as well. There were three crime intelligence and collation experts and uniform staff was used later on to monitor listening devices and telephone intercepts.

My brother John Noonan, Senior Detectives Jim O'Brien and Col Ryan, all had extensive backgrounds with the Peirces, Pentigills, Allens, Houghton, McEvoy, Farrell, Abdullah and a multitude of supporting cast, having worked on them at Richmond among, other tasking units.

Most of the detectives were very skilled, conscientious and hard men who deserved to be at the forefront of the planning and involved in the arrests and interviews of the suspects.

I've no doubt that if you placed any number of people into such a stressful and time-consuming investigation, there'd inevitably be conflict at times. And there was more conflict than we needed, due to the actions of a couple in particular.

We did the leg work and what we considered the boring shit that had to be done. For instance, we had to find and personally speak to over 5,000 taxi drivers in Victoria, to see if any had picked up any offenders from near the scene in Walsh Street South Yarra. I think at that stage most were of Greek and Italian descent and my being trained to drink in around eight languages, which included Greek and Italian, made my input invaluable.

We transcribed listening device and telephone intercept tape recordings of which there were some 1,700. Each went for about an hour and was transcribed by professional transcription personnel. We then got their transcripts and had to check, double and triple check each recording. Most tapes would be listened to for anything up to four hours each. If anything interesting was gleaned from these recordings, it was passed on to John Noonan for his assessment and follow up enquiries.

I performed witness protection on the star witness Witness X during the period she was first brought into protection and whilst she made her extensive and numerous statements. This lasted for about four and a half weeks and really opened our eyes to what low lives they were.

We conducted almost one hundred raids on suspects and associates during the investigation and did some very dangerous jobs as well. I don't have the photographic memory for the details of the job like some of the team had.

Some of the tales are humorous, shocking, infuriating, incomprehensible and some incredibly sad.

So this was the commencement of the Walsh Street Murder Investigation Task Force and my part in it. There is more detailed coverage about Walsh Street later on that fills in the job and the result for those who don't know.

As I wasn't born a super sleuth, I had to actually work my way through the uniform and CIB years before managing to crack it into the Major Crime Squad. It might be timely to take you back to the start and explain what other adventures and misadventures I endured to make it to the dizzy heights I reached.

CHAPTER THREE

The Academy

I joined the Victoria Police Force in 1981 and went through the academy in Glen Waverley in the south eastern suburbs of Melbourne. I was 18 years of age and weighed 69 kilos soaking wet. I'd joined the police force to continue a strong family presence, as my brother John Noonan was in the job, as was another relative, Frank Noonan. John was working in uniform when I joined, and Frank was a law instructor at the police academy.

I had finished my Higher School Certificate when I was 16 and worked in the ANZ Bank for a year while I waited to join 'the job' as it was referred to then and still today. I considered myself to be of above average intelligence as I had done very well academically and achieved excellent results in my final year. I was offered places at three universities to study Law or Economics and Politics. I duly passed them up as I could think of nothing worse than spending another four years studying.

I applied for the police force, sat my exams and miraculously passed. But not without having to sweat out the acceptance.

I remember coming home that day after the exams and telling my father how easy they were. He asked me to tell him about some of the questions. I told him there were the basic English grammar, spelling, punctuation, as well as some ridiculous questions, like where were the statues of the Twelve Apostles. Dad asked me what I'd answered and I laughed and said it was multiple choice. One choice was Victoria, another was Jerusalem and two others, I can't remember now. Anyway, I kept up my big smile and said, 'Where else would the statue of the 12 apostles be? Jerusalem.'

The old man sat at the kitchen table with his extremely well-muscled forearms from years as a brick layer crossed in front of his big frame. The colour red spread quickly over his face and head and his mouth turned tightly into a grimace. When this happened, I knew something was up and that I'd most probably be berated for some blatant act of stupidity I'd committed, but I had no idea what it was.

He spoke through his tight lips and gritted teeth and said in his loud and fatherly tone, 'You stupid bastard. How the bloody hell did you say they were in Jerusalem?'

There were some nuances the old man had in his pronunciation, especially when he wanted me to get the idea I'd buggered something up. The word 'stupid' was pronounced with a stretched-out emphasis on the U which made it sound like there were about four of them together instead of one. The word 'bloody' was one of his favourites and somehow he got his tongue to hang on to the letter L for a few seconds before moving on to do the same with the O's. So if I wasn't as clever as I thought I was, I'd spell the two words as Stuuuupid and Blllllloody.

I looked completely shocked and repeated more as a question than a statement, in a little less confident manner, 'Where else would the statues of the bloody 12 apostles be? Jerusalem.'

He replied, 'You dickhead. There're up off the Great Ocean Road, right up the other side of Geelong.' He shook his head sideways and said, 'Well you've buggered that up. There's no bloody way you'll get in the police force with stupid bloody answers like that. Dickhead.'

Again, the word dickhead was one of his favourites and that came out like someone had ignited the letters D and I and they overshadowed all other letters to follow. I sat there dumbfounded. How was I supposed to know they were on the Great Ocean Road? I'd never seen the bloody statues and with my strong Catholic upbringing, I thought that anything to do with the apostles had to be in Jerusalem. I couldn't believe it. It had to be bullshit and he was winding me up.

I said, 'Yeah right pap.'

I gave a half-hearted chuckle and eagerly awaited his response. Dad looked at me again and started to laugh and said, 'You stupid bastard'. In between his breaking up with laughter and his head shaking, he went on to explain to me that the 12 apostles were rock formations that were called the 12 Apostles. They weren't lifelike sculptures of them. I was amazed. I then started to nervously chuckle along with him until the lightbulb flashed on top of my head. I was overcome with dread and foreboding. What if I'd stuffed up everything else that I'd thought was easy and I get knocked back? Oh shit. What had I done?

Luckily, dad settled down and stopped laughing at me and we went through the other questions and he confirmed I'd done well with everything, excepting those treacherous bastards from Jerusalem. I never forgot that lesson and when I eventually saw those bloody statues years later, I couldn't help but mutter curses to them from the lookout for making me look like a dickhead.

Anyway, into the Academy I went and fronted up the first day in a very nervous and apprehensive mood. We soon got sorted out and organised into our squads. I was to be part of Squad 3 of 1981 and was decked out in some shitty, ill-fitting clothes they accurately called 'fatigues'. They were grey in colour and comprised of a pair of trousers and a jacket made of a drill fabric. We were issued blue uniform shirts without the police insignia badge. That would be attached on graduation. We also got a pair of parade boots and a pair of dress shoes and a white police hat without the badge. When we all got dressed into our fatigues for the first time, I thought we resembled a squad of American Milk Men from the '50s.

We all had regulation short back and sides and had to be clean shaven every day. I was among the youngest in the squad, but not the youngest. We had a few blokes that'd been through the police cadets or 'grubs' as they were known. We had a pretty good group and the time in the academy went quickly. One of the only dramas I had was one of the drill instructors taking a dislike to me from the first day. He was also the baton twirler in the police band as it turned out. I remember I was sweeping up the mess hall after a senior squad had just graduated and he walked over to me and leaned his face in close to mine and said in a malevolent tone, 'What are you doing recruit?'

I showed him the broom in my hands and replied, 'Sweeping the floor. Senior.'

He said, 'What are you some sort of smartarse Noonan?'

I knew I had to keep stone faced so I didn't reveal the contempt I had for him and said, 'No Senior.'

He stayed in my face and continued speaking through his thin lips and had his top row of teeth clamped against the bottom row, 'Don't think you're going to get any special treatment because your uncle's a law instructor Noonan. That doesn't make one piece of shit difference to me. Do you understand that Noonan?'

I replied, 'He's not my uncle but yes Senior.'

He ended with, 'Right smartarse. You're on defaulters.'

He then smiled his evil smile and walked off. Defaulters weren't good and it meant you had to stay back and do extra crap duty when everyone else went home on a Friday. We were told if you got five defaulters, you'd get the arse from the academy and that was your career over. I managed to get five in my first month, thanks to my newfound friendship with the baton twirler who kept riding me.

When he gave me the fifth one, I was told to report to the superintendent's office. Again, I thought my police career was over before it got started. They were going to kick me out of the academy and I'd be ridiculed and branded a failure for the rest of my life.

I presented to the super's office and snapped to attention and waited for him to say something. He told me to sit down and then very earnestly enquired as to why I was up to five defaulters so quickly. I explained that the baton twirler, although I didn't call him that to the boss, had taken a personal dislike to me and if he checked he would notice that all my defaulters were issued by him.

Luckily for me the superintendent was a good bloke and when I explained what the go was he told me to relax and he got Frank Noonan to come in while I was there. He told him what the baton twirler had done and Frank explained that for some reason, the nasty little prick didn't like him and was obviously trying to annoy Frank by harassing me. Whatever happened after that meeting, he lay off me and had to content himself with looking daggers at me whenever I was within range.

We marched, ran, swam and learned the law at a frenetic pace and it was most enjoyable in the main. Our drill instructor was Sergeant Graeme Puls. He looked the quintessential drill instructor from the movies. He had the ramrod straight back, the immaculate uniform, the chiselled jaw line and spoke through as small a gap between his teeth as he could. He sounded like a menacing ventriloquist doll and had piercing eyes.

He took a shine to me and would regularly march up to me on parade and stand right in front of me. He'd lean in with his face so close I initially thought he was going to kiss me. Then he'd scream at me for some marching misdemeanour and do his best to land one liners on me. This was to make me look stupid and he no doubt thought his conduct would intimidate me.

Initially it did. But the more familiar I became with his quirky sense of humour, I realised he was a good bloke and he mellowed his hardwood veneer.

He used to produce a piece of cardboard on morning parade and run it along the face of some unsuspecting recruit. If it made a noise, that recruit was yelled at and may have defaulters. He'd have to shave more closely so the cardboard didn't scream the news to the drilly that his shave wasn't close enough. The first time the cardboard dobbed me in, I was actually quite pleased because that meant I needed to shave. It wasn't something I did so I felt like a real boy.

The tallest bloke in the squad was Frank Van Der Horst, who was one of the 'grubs' which was an irreverent term given to the police cadets. He was 6 feet 4 or so and built like a beanpole. He was made the right marker. That meant everyone else had to line up off him on parade and during marching drills. Frank would regularly go left when ordered to right wheel or vice versa. He'd then incur the wrath of Sergeant Puls receiving the in your face shouting routine.

It was one of his verbal attacks on Frank that led to his demise as the hardnosed drilly and let everyone see there was actually a bloke with a keen sense of humour in there. Frank had done something wrong that morning on parade and Puls pounced. As he yelled at him from point blank range, Frank answered his question with some smart-arse remark which I found hilarious.

I burst out laughing from just a couple of spots down the ranks. Puls was like a mozzie to a fat kid's leg. He executed a perfect turn and marched up to me. He leaned in and started yelling some derogatory remark at me. I couldn't contain myself and was laughing in his face with tears running from my eyes, as he continued his tirade. After what seemed like an eternity, he stopped yelling. I think he realised I was gone and nothing he could scream at me was going to bring me back. He stood there glaring at me. I managed to momentarily straighten my face.

He said, 'Is there something wrong with you Noonan?'

That was it. Off I went and burst out laughing again right in his face. I think this caught him unawares and he battled to contain himself from joining me. He started to go red in the face with the effort and when I was sure he was going to crack, he executed an about face. In doing so, he overbalanced and had to take a sideways step to correct his stance. He turned and looked at me with a grin spreading across his leather-like face and spat out, 'I stepped on a stone. Didn't I Noonan?'

I burst out laughing again and he joined me before turning and walking away so we didn't see him do it. As he turned to walk away he mumbled to me, 'You're a fucking idiot Noonan.' It wasn't said with any malice and it was his way of acknowledging I was a funny bastard.

I came across Sergeant Graeme Puls again years later when I was living in Papua New Guinea where I was working as a Special Investigator for the Prime Minister's Department investigating corruption. He was working as a Police Advisor to the PNG Constabulary. If he thought we were hard to get through to in the old days, he was in for a shock in PNG. He still had the chiselled jaw and was very funny talking about these days at the academy. Unfortunately, he passed away late in 2018 as I found out when it was mentioned on a Police Veterans website. I didn't know until after he had been buried. I probably would not have attended anyway as I have an aversion to police funerals and find them too distressing.

We did boxing and firearms training and I found all this to be very interesting and it was great to finally fire the Smith & Wesson 38 calibre revolvers when the time came. One of the firearms instructors always spoke in a staccato manner I associated more with the military than the coppers. He'd yell things with his Scottish accent and would pause after each second or third word which would be accentuated with a rise in pitch and then drop again at the commencement of the next three word sentence. I think it was an attempt to make everything he said sound important and was very useful in keeping us awake. Sean Connery did this regularly in his movies and every time he did it I thought of that drilly.

I remember at the end of our time in the academy, this bloke had mellowed and yelled, 'Always fire a warning shot Noonan. Just make sure it hits the same spot as the first shot.'

It took us a couple of minutes to figure this out and we smiled our understanding. He then turned serious and said, 'Don't laugh boys. Stay alive and look after yourselves. Remember it's better to be judged by 12 than carried by six.'

That wasn't to be the only time I heard that saying and it's amazing how that advice would come back to me in later years. We were by no means marksmen but we were reasonably competent in the use of the Smith & Wesson revolver. I had no real idea what he was talking about and thought he was trying to scare us with these dire warnings. I now realise in full what he told us and wonder whether some police were to take his warning literally in years to come.

We had a good laugh and learned a lot in the academy and were all very pleased to graduate in June of 1981. Two blokes from our sister squad got sacked in the last week for going to the pub and getting caught. We couldn't believe it. Sacked with three days to go before graduation. They were heartbroken and had to leave that day after handing back all their gear. After graduating and seeing some of the things 'real coppers' did, I thought the treatment of those blokes was harsh.

The only other bloke to get the arse from our two squads was a bloke who shared my room for a while. He'd been back squadded due to an alleged knee injury and came into our squad and ended up sharing my room. He was from the bush and was a different sort of bloke. I wasn't to know how different until I was again summoned to the superintendent's office. I hadn't had any more defaulters, so I was at a loss to understand what I'd done. I walked in and was told to take a seat. The super asked me how well I knew my roommate and whether I'd seen or heard him doing anything strange. I told the super I knew he was supposed to have a bung knee but that was it. I really didn't have much to do with him. He wasn't one of the blokes I knocked around with.

He asked me again if I'd seen him do anything strange or odd in our room. I repeated I hadn't and was starting to feel like I'd done something wrong. After a while the questions stopped and he sat there looking at me. I excused myself and asked him what this was about. It turned out that my roommate had been defecating into brown paper bags and mailing them to people. He'd also been using his recruit shirt to get half priced McDonalds on the weekends, pretending to be a real policeman.

I was astounded. Then I started laughing. The super didn't think it was very appropriate and asked what I was laughing about. I told him I thought he was having a lend of me and what he'd told me couldn't be right. He didn't smile or lighten up in the slightest and reaffirmed what he'd said.

My roommate was gone by the time I went back to my room. The thing that got me was that he'd been sacked from the academy and let go. I couldn't believe that someone who did what he did, wouldn't be charged with something and end up with a record of what a sick bastard he must've been.

Anyway, after the demise of these blokes the rest of us graduated and became real policeman. To add insult to injury, all the marching we'd done counted for bugger all, as it rained the entire week and we had to have our Graduation Ceremony in the Police Chapel.

CHAPTER FOUR

My First Uniform Station

After the Academy we had to select what stations we wanted as training stations. I selected suburbs all near home in the south eastern suburbs of Melbourne. I was shocked when I got notified that my training station would be City West. I'd never heard of it and when I found out it was in William Street in the city I couldn't believe it. I had to leave home and I moved into a flat in Toorak with a couple of blokes from my squad. Funnily enough one was our right marker Mr Frank Van Der Horst.

I spent two years at City West and worked with some really good blokes and some not so good blokes as well. It was an awakening getting to a real police station and going out in a real divisional van, armed with a real gun. The training was over. Now it was time for the real deal.

The agenda for my first station involved the introduction to three things that were alien to me. But three things that would stay with me forever: the grog, guns and violence.

My first shift was with a tough sergeant by the name of Ross Indian or better known as The Chief, for obvious reasons. I had to drive him around for the day in silence. He was really quiet as it turned out but was rumoured to be good with his fists and not one to argue with. As I was still a less than strapping lad, weighing 69kg with something like three per cent body fat, I was in no shape to argue with anyone, let alone this bloke. Every time I went to speak to him during that shift he'd glare at me and say, 'Did I talk to you?' That was my cue to shut up and look and listen.

At the end of the shift I got changed and was quietly relieved to get away. It's very uncomfortable spending a day wanting to ask every stupid question that popped into my head and realising I had to shut up and only speak when spoken to.

As I was talking to one of the other new constables, who again was Frank Van Der Horst, The Chief walked past in his civilian clothes and stopped and looked at me.

'Where are you going?' he asked.

'Home sergeant,' I said.

'No you're not. It's your shout for a beer. That's what happens on your first day constable.'

'I don't drink much sergeant,' I said.

'I don't give a rat's arse how much you drink. I drink shit loads and you have to buy them,' he said.

So that was that. Off we went to one of the many local watering holes in the North Melbourne area and I bought round after round and drank beer after beer. I don't remember exactly what happened during the course of the night with all my new work colleagues but I remember waking up in the bed at the City West Police Station and feeling like I'd been hit by a truck. I didn't remember what I'd done or how I got there and where 'there' was.

I walked out of the little room where the bed was kept for just this purpose, or more correctly for coppers working a quick changeover and not wanting to drive home. I felt like I'd been hit with a baseball bat. My temple was throbbing . My eyes felt like they had ground glass in them. My throat was dry as a chip and I had a headache the likes of which I'd never experienced before.

This was my most memorable hangover in my brief drinking career. I didn't know whether I wanted to be sick, lie down, stand up or shoot myself.

Anyway, I walked in to the mess room whilst still in the process of trying to understand what I was doing and there was The Chief and a few of the other blokes that I'd been buying copious amounts of beer for the night before. I was greeted more warmly than I expected.

It was the start of a career of working hard and playing hard, which meant that my daily intake of beer went through the roof and unfortunately I took to it like a duck to water. That was the culture of the police force and I'd just been christened. There was always someone to drink with and always somewhere to drink it. Whether it was a pub, park or the roof of the City West Police Station. There was always somewhere.

Luckily for my health, I very quickly got a lot better at the drinking caper and managed to get to a stage where I could back up day after day without feeling as bad as I did on the day I had my alcoholic cherry popped.

I think that was one of the problems. I compared every hangover to that first one and when I didn't hit those sickening heights, I felt like I'd won something, rather than lost a few million more brain cells. Like golf, football, cricket or whatever else, drinking required practise and I got plenty. I really put in the hard yards and as it turned out I was considered a reasonably funny bastard on the turps. This made me popular on the circuit after whatever shift I was on whether that be morning, noon or night.

CHAPTER FIVE

The Duty Officer Driver

Even when I would've laid London to a brick I wouldn't be called upon to drink, the unexpected would jump up and bite me on the arse. Not long after the initiation with The Chief, I was rostered to work night shift and I was to be the Duty Officer driver. I had to ask some of the more experienced coppers that spoke to me what this role entailed. I was informed it meant driving the inspector all over the district like a chauffeur and being a general dog's body.

The inspector on that night shift turned out to be a bloke we'll call Big Red. He was a rather large and well-built gentleman with red hair and what looked a frightening demeanour for a young pup like me.

I picked him up at Russell Street Police Station and he shook my hand, nearly snapping my fingers off in the process. I always shook hard, as the old man had drilled into us. It didn't matter at that stage, as Big Red's hands were like vices, as were his habits. As I was to learn the hard way. I drove him around the inner-city stations and followed him in like a puppy, as he checked the station crews were on deck and doing what they were supposed to do.

At about 1.30am on the first night after we'd cleared Carlton, I asked him where to next. He said get back to Russell Street and park underneath. We might be tied up for a while. I did as directed and followed him into Russell Street to one of the offices there.

As I walked in I noticed there were other inspectors, senior sergeants, detectives and God knows who else. I felt very uncomfortable all of a sudden. I was the only young bloke there and I'm sure I was the most junior person ever to have set foot in that particular office. Big Red knew everyone and those he hadn't seen for a while he gave the grip of death.

There were some big boys and they handled his grip without any apparent discomfort. I was expecting to be banished to the Russell Street uniform tearoom, but instead he introduced me and made me feel part of it.

Then next thing I knew was I had a Vitamin B can in my hand and Big Red said 'cheers'. I don't remember how many times that word was repeated, but it didn't take long for me to end up fly blown and wanting to curl up and go to sleep. Everyone else was dropping cans like Prohibition was coming into force the next day.

I was no match and fell by the wayside only to be woken up at some stage later in the morning. Big Red didn't even look like he'd had a beer and I didn't know whether that was because he could handle his grog, or maybe he'd stopped drinking hours before when I'd come to an unexpectedly early demise.

He woke me up and helped me down to the car and asked me if I was right to drive. Blood alcohol levels weren't a big deal in those days and coppers enjoyed a fair leeway. I got in the police car and tried to reverse out of the car park. I couldn't manage to coordinate too well and it didn't take long before I was told to stop and get out. I was assisted into the passenger seat and he drove me.

I was supposed to drive him home and then take the car back to City West and knock off from there. As it turned out, he drove me home after having to wake me up continuously and ask directions. I reckon this was the first time I experienced having to try and wake myself from what seemed like a coma. Every time he woke me, I'd sit bolt upright like I'd just been tapped on the arse in a gay bar. Then I had to try and remember where I was, whilst blinking rapidly trying to get the optics to focus.

The hardest part then turned out to be speaking the English language in a manner that he could understand. It was like my tongue had a weight tied to it and the harder I tried to coordinate my thinking to my talking, the worse it sounded. As a navigator I was bloody hopeless.

I don't know what happened after he dropped me off at my flat and relieved me of my service revolver, radio and kit bag. I was apologising and felt like I'd let the team down. He was very understanding and told me to get to bed and hopefully I'd be a better driver next time I took him out.

I was relieved of that duty the next night and one of the other older blokes took over. I was never so happy to be back on the van. He'd destroyed me in quick time, but I never forgot what a good bloke he was. I had contact with him right through my career and he ended up assisting the coroner, Hal Hallenstein, during the Police Shootings Enquiry, which I was called to attend after I had resigned from the police force in 1991.

I remember one of the funniest blokes I have ever had the pleasure to meet was Col Florence, who at this stage was a sergeant at City West and would later be my senior sergeant at the Major Crime Squad. Col always had and still does have a perpetual smile on his face and loved fishing and drinking. One afternoon, just for something different, we went to a pub with Flo and a heap of other blokes.

As tended to happen regularly, it turned into a huge session. Flo got into an impromptu drinking competition with one of the other blokes that included the consumption of numerous shots and mixed drinks, which in those days was highly unusual as beer was the usual poison of choice. Steve 'Jossa' Jostlear was a big, strong Senior Constable who could drink like a fish and fight like a thrashing machine. He was only in his mid to late twenties and would have had a good 10 years on Flo. The end result was the pair of them ended up maggoted. They sat unable to drink anything for an hour or so before it was decided we better get them home. It was the early hours of the morning by this stage and he had well and truly earned his stripes. The poor old publican had done the same as he was regularly called on to stay back and serve these reprobates who had sworn to protect and serve. I think it was more like they wanted to protect him so he could serve them. I somehow got volunteered to drive Flo home.

We assisted him out to his ute and he was chattering away incoherently. He was unsteady on his feet and had to be physically assisted into the passenger seat by a couple of blokes. As he was plonked in the seat, one of the blokes slammed the door and I walked around and got into the driver's seat. Col was trying to tell me something and was laughing and then grimacing in obvious pain. I did a quick check and couldn't find anything untoward. I thought he had his left arm extended holding on the safety handle or Jesus Bar above the door. It was called the Jesus Bar in a police car because during hairy pursuits the passenger would have no recourse but to try and prevent being thrown around the front of the divvy van or sedan, than to hold onto the bar with both hands and yell Jesus regularly, normally on cornering at 300 miles per hour or when just missing another car or pole.

He kept mumbling and slurring and was obviously still in pain. So I got out of the car and walked around to check more thoroughly from his side. As I got to his door, I noticed three and a bit fingers protruding from the top of the closed door jam. Once I realised what had happened, I opened the door and released Flo's hand. I checked to see if his fingers were broken and by some miracle, they seemed to be alright. He was relieved to have his fingers out of the door and mumbled and slurred more contentedly than before.

Another one of the blokes led the way in his car as he knew where Flo lived, and he was going to drive me back after we delivered him safely home. We pulled up out the front of his house and got him out of the car. We straightened up his clothes and he seemed to be speaking more coherently. That was no doubt due to not drinking for a while and the pain from his fingers which he continued to massage. He assured us he would be alright and off he went inside the front door after taking an inordinate amount of time trying to get the key in the lock. He was still in his blue uniform trousers and police shirt and had a jacket over the top as a clever disguise when we all went to the pub in nearly identical attire. We waited out the front for a few minutes to make sure his wife didn't wake up and go off tap. She was a top lady and Flo lovingly called her Digger. They are still together today and she has certainly lived up to her nickname having stayed in the trenches with Flo for so many decades.

We were about to drive off when Flo came stumbling out his front door after us and got straight into the back seat of the car.

'What are you doing Flo?' I said.

He looked at us like a rabbit caught in the headlights and had somehow sobered up remarkably quickly in such a short time frame.

'I took my jacket off and was trying to get undressed as quietly as I could so I didn't wake up the cook,' he said. 'I got my boots off and was undoing the last button on my shirt when she woke up. She said she had not heard me come home and asked if I was on early shift. I didn't know what to say. I stood up and started doing my buttons up again. I told her I got home early and she was already asleep so I slept in the lounge room so I didn't wake her up. I didn't have the guts to tell her I'd just got home. So, I got dressed and said bye bye and walked out to go to work.'

He then burst out laughing in his characteristic laugh which was impossible not to laugh with. And we certainly did. I laughed that hard I couldn't talk. We drove him back to the police station arriving about 6am. We helped him into the bedroom and put him to bed still in his uniform. He was on a day off that day but had to stay at the office and get driven home again at the completion of his pretend shift. Both he and Joss were crook as dogs and both had to endure every long minute of that day.

CHAPTER SIX

Run, The Transvestite's Got a Comb!

As I was to learn the hard way, City West had within is geographical area some of the roughest, toughest pubs in Melbourne in the 1980s. After graduation, I felt like every time I put on that uniform, I was bullet proof and never thought of getting the crap belted out of me. It didn't take long for me to learn that we were merely flesh and blood and I was surprised how much blood we actually possessed.

One of my most memorable outings on the van was with a little angry man by the name of Barry. He was short and wiry, with a hair lip and one of the worst outlooks on life of anyone I'd met. Even though his outlook was nasty, he could be remarkably funny, even if he wasn't trying to be.

I remember working the afternoon shift divvy van one day when at about 10pm we were called to a brawl at the Royal Exchange Hotel in Victoria Street. Up to that point, I'd never been unlucky enough to actually go inside that den of iniquity and cesspool of sub-humanity. It was a shit hole for those who don't know what a den or a cesspool is.

Barry had spent most of the shift trying to cram as much police knowledge into my head as he could. He was very matter of fact and spoke with a higher pitched voice. I think he was so pissed off at the world because he was short and had a hair lip. Fair enough too. Whatever his motivation he was sure as hell one grumpy prick.

That night on the way to the brawl he told me to stick with him and don't wander off or I could get the shit belted out of me. So we pull up out the front of this so called pub and jump out of the van with Barry leading our two man charge into the bowels of that less than salubrious establishment.

We walked through the solid wooden doors into an open bar area that I couldn't believe. It had a bare concrete floor with metal tables and chairs that were actually bolted to the floor. I later asked Barry why they were bolted down and he told me it so the patrons couldn't use them as weapons during a blue. I looked from the tables and chairs to the bar. It was also made of concrete with a steel roller shutter closing off the bar from the public area.

I thought the joint was shut until I saw the rather large barman serving VB cans thought the grills in the shutter to one of the punters. I thought I'd walked into a pub straight out of *The Flintstones.*

The customers were a very mixed bunch of social detritus from a multitude of ethnic origins. There were Aboriginals, Maoris, Samoans, Tongans and Caucasians of various origins. Most were male and weighed probably two to three times more than both Barry and I put together. There were some there that it was alleged were female of some description, but I was extremely dubious.

Next thing Barry walks away from me and goes to the top of the bar area, further into the bowels of the beast. I stood there trying to look authoritarian and masculine while my skinny legs were hopefully not too obvious in the rhythmic banging in my rather roomy uniform trousers.

A few of the patrons who were absolutely shit faced took the opportunity to mumble some less than complementary remarks and I'm sure one said something about rooting me, but I chose to ignore this. Although I must say it does cause an involuntary clinching of the cheeks of your arse when some 30 stone Maori mentions perhaps trying to mount you.

So I'm standing there doing the 'Right O, right O' my old man used to say when we were getting a little out of line at a family gathering. I used my deepest voice and tried to push what little chest I had out the front of my shirt.

I was wondering where the bloody hell Barry was when I heard a scream and then out he flies with some form of she-man creature in high heels and a dress in hot pursuit. He was being chased by something holding something out in front of him. This was before the days of political correctness and I apologise to the LGBTQIA community for our lack of tact and understanding. But I can't rewrite history to placate the present so that's that.

Barry runs past me and yells 'Run. I think he's got a knife.'

That was good enough for me and I actually overtook him just as we went through the doors at Mach 9. I ran straight ahead towards the Victoria Market and Barry went right and was running along the top of William Street. Thank God he kept pursuing Barry and was yelling out how he was going to kill the little fucker when he got hold of him.

I ran back to the van and was trying to get the key in the door to get on the radio when out came some of my new friends from inside the pub. It seemed the key and the door lock had both shrunk and do you reckon I could get the bloody thing open? It gave me a stronger appreciation of when people are shit scared in movies and everyone wonders why they can't get the key in the lock. I think there must be a nerve that runs from your arse to your fingers that in times of terror cause the fingers to fail.

A couple came at me and started pushing me whilst I continued to try and get into the bloody van. I managed to open the passenger door and grab hold of the microphone from the cradle mounted on the dashboard.

I was dragged out of the van and was starting to get hit by one or more of the drunken rowdy mob that was now foaming at the chance of a free hit on an under resourced young copper. I was fending off punches and in doing so I was kicked in the guts and was hit multiple times in quick succession. I hit the deck and a couple were now starting to lay in the boots.

It's funny that at the time you don't register pain, or I didn't on this occasion. It was more like being a witness to events than feeling like you were in it. I was obviously scared and trying to defend myself and had not thought of attack. I would not have made a dent in these blokes anyway. Years later after numerous hidings I did try and take the initiative and if things looked grim get in quick and do whatever I could to disable my potential attackers.

I don't know whether I consciously tried to roll over the kerb and gutter and under the passenger side of the van. Somehow, I'd kept hold of the radio and as I was either kicked or fled under the van. I found they were actually kicking the bottom of the van rather than me, as their access was partially blocked by the gutter being close to the van. For once being a skinny bastard was an advantage, as I was able to somehow slip between the two.

I realised I still had a death grip on the microphone and was actually depressing the button that opened the microphone. So other police units could hear my mob of admirers yelling their abuse at me as they were fluffing their new pillows. Me!

Some of the other City West coppers that turned up to our rescue reckoned they could hear me grunting and the sounds of me getting belted through the open microphone. When I twigged what was happening, I released the button and then heard the D24 operator calling for the unit in trouble.

I nearly swallowed the mic in my hurry to blurt out that I was in deep shit. I pushed the button and yelled, 'City West 303, police in trouble at the Royal Exchange.'

I then heard the D24 operator calling for any unit to assist City West 303, Police in Trouble at the Royal Exchange.

The old time dimension was in slow motion and I almost found it amusing that these dumb arses couldn't get me whilst I sought refuge under the van. It seemed instantaneous that I heard the sound of police sirens screaming their message that the cavalry was on their way. I'd never called up police in trouble and it was the one call that caused all coppers within the area and sometimes beyond, to drop whatever they were doing and rush helter skelter to the scene of the drama.

Even though I'd lost every round of this bout so far, I remember smiling to myself that these coppers were coming to save me. That's a feeling I'll never forget. I was part of the police force and they sure looked after each other.

Police cars arrived one after the other and it was on for young and old. The more coppers that turned up, the more drunken crooks that came out of the pub and joined in the fray. I managed to use the distraction to roll out from under the van on the driver's side and went to assist my saviours.

We ended up getting the better of one of the biggest Maoris and there were about five of us trying to get him into the rear of one of the vans. He was strong as an ox and he kept trading blows with whoever he could hit. He was hit multiple times as well and I remember loading up a big right and belting him right in the head. As soon as I hit him I felt a pain shoot through my hand and I thought I'd hit a brick wall. Due to an unhealthy dose of adrenalin coursing through my veins, it hurt but it wasn't serious enough to withdraw.

This bloke was belted with batons, fists and even a baton torch and still we couldn't get him to budge. Then somehow, he managed to turn himself around and sat on the lip of the rear door of the van and continued to fight. Someone hit him over the head again and it did nothing. Then someone yelled 'Don't hit him in the head. Hit him in the balls.'

So someone loads up a baton blow to his nuts and he barely flinched. He took another few full on nut crackers before his grip weakened enough to be forced into the van and the door was slammed shut and padlocked. There were coppers everywhere locking up crooks and the fighting seemed to stop once our bloke was finally lodged in the van.

It was only then that I thought I'd better find Barry.

He came walking back towards our van and was sweating like a pig, excuse the pun. I asked him if he was alright and he said he was. I asked him where the sheila that was chasing him was. He said not to worry about it.

We took our bloke to the City Watch House, as City West didn't have cells and organised for a crew and a half to be there when we opened the door of the van. I couldn't believe it. Out pops this humungous head full of black curly hair with the huge Maori smiling at us and he says, 'It's OK Bro. I won't cause no more trouble, hey.'

Even so the six or so coppers there stood at the ready as this bloke was chaperoned into the watch house and put through the book. He was charged with multiple counts of Assault Police, Assault in Company and Drunk. Due to him being as pissed as 20 men he couldn't be interviewed about the assaults and really didn't need to be. Nothing he could say would change the circumstances and the damage he'd done on his rampage.

I finally relaxed when we got to the watch house and once the adrenalin started to subside, the pain started to come to the fore.

My ribs were sore as buggery and my hand had swollen up and was obviously broken.

Before I went to get treated for my injuries, we gathered back at the City West Police Station for a check on how everyone ended up. Barry was asking me all the way back if I was OK and I was telling him I thought I'd broken my hand. He was asking me what had happened and I filled him in.

I asked him how he got on with the crazy sheila chasing him and he told me not to worry about it. I couldn't understand why he wouldn't tell me what'd happened, but I was neither senior nor well acquainted with him to keep asking.

When we walked back into the station there were the other two crews there with the sergeant and I think a couple of other units from surrounding stations who'd come to our rescue. We were warmly greeted and the sergeant immediately asked me if I was OK. He inspected my injuries and told me I'd have to go to hospital and get checked out.

While we had a cup of tea in the mess room, one of the other coppers from City West saw Barry and started laughing at him. Barry was full on pissed off at being laughed at and I couldn't understand what the drama was. I soon found out the cause of the levity.

It turned out the crazy sheila who chased him with a knife out of the pub was a six-feet-something transvestite we'll call Bridie, who was well known to everyone there. He or she apparently still had the male tackle but had been on hormones for 18 months on her way to getting a tackle box instead.

Apparently, she was a really nasty bastard when pissed and had a hatred of him from some multiple dealings in the past. He used to do assault and robberies on anyone he could get hold of and was a very strong and dangerous crook, or crookette.

It also turned out that the flick knife I thought Bridie was brandishing was a fold up pocket comb. I started laughing, as did everyone else when the Senior Connie dropped the full story.

They'd seen Barry running away from him and had interrupted and bailed him up against the wall of a building. Barry came back to them telling them to be careful as Bridie had a knife. He produced the flick comb and was berating Barry for running away from a lady with a comb.

The other blokes cracked up laughing and Bridie also got cuffed and slotted for drunk. Barry didn't want him charged with Assault Police as he was too embarrassed with the reality rather than the perception of the situation and threat. Everyone hung that much shit on the poor bloke he ended up telling them to get fucked and wouldn't go for a beer after work. He apparently cracked it and got changed and went home.

I was taken to the police hospital in South Melbourne which was situated behind the now demolished Prince Henry's Hospital in St Kilda Road. Wherever it was, I had my ribs and hand strapped as there wasn't much they could do for either at that time. I had to go for x-rays the next day and that's when my ribs were found to be only bruised and my metacarpal bone was broken, as was my little finger on my right hand. I had also sustained a broken nose but luckily it was broken straight and didn't have to be reset. I had two black eyes, I think from the broken nose and numerous scrapes, cuts and bruises from my forced retreat under the van.

I had a couple of days off and was sore for more than that with the rib and hand injury. That was my first police in trouble. That was the first time I had been kicked in my life, as it wasn't the done thing, especially when they were on the ground. It was my first injury on duty.

It was the harsh realisation that the police uniform didn't provide some miraculous protection from physical injury. I remember looking at the shirt from that night and it had bitumen stains and tears on the back and one sleeve. It had blood all over the front and had one of the front breast pockets torn off. I showed it to my flat mate when I eventually got home and he thought it was great.

Deep down I actually thought it was pretty cool too. I felt like I had somehow earned a right of passage that night.

It was circumstances like that night that form a very strong bond between coppers. The sounds of those sirens coming to our aid were the best sounds I'd ever heard. It wouldn't be the last time I got the crap belted out of me, injured or came up police in trouble.

CHAPTER SEVEN

St Kilda Police Force

On 24 November 1983 I reported for duty at the St Kilda Police Station in Carlisle Street. I knew a few blokes at St Kilda and so it was better than my first day at City West when I didn't know anyone or anything. In the two and a half years since I had graduated, I'd learnt a fair bit about what to do and how to do it. I'd got more than my fair share of crooks at City West and had a good grounding for taking the next step in my career. St Kilda had a certain aura about it with a fair few people I'd spoken to, saying they were a bunch of cowboys who thought they were better than everyone else.

I was still a strapping 69kg, just on 6 feet tall, and was shaving every day whether I had to or not. I could drink like a thrashing machine and enjoyed being sociable. On that first day I was allocated my locker which was the old style 5 feet high steel locker with a vent near the top of the door and the handle in the middle. The locker room was an old portable at the rear of the police station. The police station itself was a two-story edifice with a staircase on the left of the entry into the watch house from the street. The Senior Sergeant and some of the administration personnel were housed up the staircase on the first floor.

The ground floor had the watch house just to the right of the entry double glass and wood trimmed swinging doors. These doors were heavy as buggery and caught many unwary crook and some coppers, on both the way in and the way out. They were like the saloon doors in Western movies except they were full length, had the glass panels and were attached to the front of a police station in Victoria rather than a saloon in Texas. Apart from those minor discrepancies they were reasonably similar.

The watch house had a front reception counter with a small desk and a chair. Just off to the right of that was the actual counter where the watch house book was kept for recording the crooks' details and taking their property off them prior to them being lodged in the cells. It also housed the firearms receptacles and the crew kits and keys for the vans and cars. The floor was concrete with some areas carpeted and some bare. The counter was made of wood and was cut out of the wall leading out to the cells, similar to a servery in a restaurant. The cells were concrete floors and walls and steel bars with a wet cell for housing dirty drunks that had been sick, drunk or had soiled themselves. This was the most sparsely furnished so it could be easily hosed down with a fire hose when it got too messed up.

The station looked like an older style house that had additions stuck on as it grew like it was a living entity. The courthouse was at the rear at the end of the short driveway that ran down the southern side of the station. The lane way had an entrance through which crooks could be unloaded from the van and taken through to the watch house and then into the cells. If you were taken to the left of the watch house foyer it normally meant you had some dramas. You were either under arrest or you were there to assist with enquiries as it is so eloquently put these days.

There was a corridor running parallel with the street off the foyer that had a couple of interview rooms and a room where there were a few desks and chairs where briefs of evidence and other paperwork could be prepared after an arrest and before court. The interview rooms were small with a couple of little wooden desks, chairs and a typewriter so we could conduct formal Records of Interview.

Now typewriters were like computers except they were not plugged in and had keys on them that had to be physically depressed for the letter to strike the paper through a typewriter ribbon, so the letter would be imprinted on the clean white sheet of paper. They were very heavy, and some crooks alleged that they were used to hit them over the head on the odd occasion. As if. They were the only means of recording an interview. Nowadays they have video with audio that records everything that is said and done. Lucky they didn't have this technology in the eighties!

These Records of Interview would be read aloud by the crook at the completion of the interview and they would be invited to sign the pages and would receive a copy. The crook would give his copy to his solicitor for court. Unless of course you were skilled or lucky enough to get a signed Statement of Confession from a crook looking for redemption or one who knew if he or she fought the charges and lost he was going to look very bad and get a longer stretch.

St Kilda was referred to as the 'unwalled asylum' by many coppers who worked there. There was always a great cross section of crooks, hookers, druggies and nuff nuffs to watch, speak to and take the piss out of. There were a lot of boarding houses, cheap motels, dodgy little shops that sold food, coffee and drugs in a package deal. You could even get your heroin home delivered at one stage with a video to fall asleep with while dribbling a mouth full of chocolate all over themselves.

It was on the first couple of days that I met some really great ladies and gentlemen and some cowboys as well.

St Kilda in those days had some of the future leaders of the Victoria Police Force as it was in those early days. Nowadays it is a department and the difference is notable. I was always in the top few crook catchers and earned my place the longer I was there. After six months in Special Duties with Mullett and Panagiotaros I took up nearly 96 offenders for just under 700 criminal offences. It got me into the Criminal Investigation Branch as the only Constable and one of the youngest at the time ever to achieve this feat. So I wasn't just a good singer I could work as well.

Some of the future luminaries were Paul Mullett, who was the future secretary of the Police Association, a Dual Valour Award winner, and Noel Ashby, who would go on to work with me at Fitzroy CIB and eventually climb the dizzy heights of Assistant Commissioner.

Some of the fish and chip shops sold $50 flake in those days. We regularly knocked over one establishment that had more druggies than a Bali prison hanging around it.

We would sit off over the road on the roof of a crappy boarding house with binoculars. As soon as we saw some shit bag hand over $20 or $50 notes, and not get any change before the bloke behind the jump leaned down under the counter and put something into the white paper that was used to wrap up that rather expensive bit of shark – and it wasn't a lemon wedge – we would make our move.

We would radio one of our other blokes who'd grab the druggie away from the shop and usually find a bit of folded silver foil in the wrapping. The dumb arses would do this one after the other and sometimes it was like shooting ducks in a pond.

CHAPTER EIGHT

If You're Lost Ask a Hooker

It was amazing to me how many blokes got lost around Fitzroy Street and Grey Street in St Kilda. It never ceased to confound my little brain how all these lost and lonely men would seek directions from hookers. Very rarely did anyone ever say they were there to buy a root. They were all lost. The drugged-up hookers must've looked like Melway's representatives. The Melways was the only source of street maps and was the only street directory issued to every police car in those days. Everyone used it and many would cite the Melways reference for invitations to everything from weddings to birthday parties. The only road they knew was the road to happiness.

If you could've seen some of these malnourished, zonked out women of all ages, staggering or tripping along the street in their high heels, ridiculously tight mini skirt and top normally opened to display their tits, it'd make you laugh.

What it wouldn't make you want to do was proposition them, pay them and take them for a root.

Although hookers, or as we called them 'crows', were mostly drug addled degenerates some of them had very strong work ethic. I remember one such hooker. She worked her arse off and other bits as well. She even worked the night she had her baby. Yes, Seriously.

BREAKING RANKS

We were on the night shift van and as we did our usual crawl around the area, we see this crow who we will call Trixie. I know her real name, but I don't want any 30-something-year-old druggie out there who has just stolen my book, learning their heroin addicted and fucked up life was their mum's fault. Trixie was in her late twenties and actually had some meat on her bones. She wasn't the typical scraggy skeleton that most of the heroin using hookers were. She had long dark hair and was of European descent and taller than average as well, so she stood out from the pack.

This night just after we hit the road at the start of our shift, we see Trixie shimmying and tripping her way along Grey Street. She had the uniform on. The tight as glad wrap mini skirt, the tank top with half her back showing and high heels you could have rappelled off. The poor bugger looked like she was walking on house bricks, she was making such a task of it. As we came level with her I nearly dropped my smoke. Her tank top and mini skirt were separated by the most pregnant of tummies sticking out like she was about to give birth to a foal. So I get the driver to pull over and we put the hazard lights on the van to let all the gutter crawlers and general scumbags know that we were going to check someone.

I recognised Trixie and realised it must have been months since I had seen her. I didn't even know she was pregnant. I would assume she had done some time in the can and must have been pregnant before going in and came out in the advanced stages. I called to her from the van and she keeps walking like a zombie with blocked ears. I had to get out of the van and grab hold of her to halt her progress. I was worried because sometimes when you interrupt their crawl it's like waking a sleepwalker. They can lose balance and go A over T onto the ground and take whoever they grab on the way down with them.

As she stops and her radar lets her know someone is holding onto her and she can't walk off, she looks at me and tries to focus. Once the penny drops and she sort of realises it is the coppers, she starts fumbling around in her little handbag for a cigarette. She manages to get one out and put it to her lips after what seemed an eternity of her pouting and pursing her lips trying to land on the end of the smoke. Somehow, she even lit it in the right end.

I brought her over to the front of the van and was trying to ask her when the last time she had used was. She kept looking at me like I was an alien and was in a full-time struggle trying to keep her eyes on me. Whether it was disinterest or dyslexia I am not sure. It reminded me of a video game where the player has to try and keep missile lock on their target whilst on the move. She was zonked off her tits on heroin. I managed to get her to dribble enough to inform me of that much. I asked her when the baby was due and she said that day. I couldn't believe it. She was due to have a baby that day and was out hawking her wares on the street full of scag (which was police talk for heroin in those days).

I called an ambulance and waited there with her until they turned up. When they did they could not believe their eyes either. They checked her over before sticking her on a stretcher and taking her off to hospital.

We shook our heads and put it down to another sick story from St Kilda. Luckily, I had not had the pleasure of being a father at this stage in my life or my reaction to what she was doing would have been angrier. When you know how precious kids are, to see someone disrespect the privilege so badly would have been too much, I think.

At about 3am we were again in between jobs and cruised up Grey Street to the exact same place we had seen Trixie before and bugger me if she wasn't back. This time the tight mini and tank top was gone and instead she was wearing a white hospital gown with her arse hanging out the rear as they are wont to do in those most ill-fitting of garments. She was in bare feet and her gown was being blown all over the shop displaying her bare arse to the world. I don't think it was the first time the world had witnessed this, but I would like to bet it was the first time in a hospital gown.

I pointed out Trixie to the van driver and he moved up Grey Street to her location. Before we got there some bloke had pulled over to the kerb and she was leaning in his window obviously discussing rates for services. We pulled up behind this car and I got out and walked up to the driver's window and asked him to get out of the car. My off sider took Trixie away from the car and was trying to talk to her. I questioned the driver and he eventually confirmed he was going to try and have sex with her. I asked him why he would want to do that when she was obviously about to give birth as well as being zonked off her tits. He told me in a whisper that he had two reasons. Firstly, he liked white women and she was a nice big one. The second reason was that he found pregnant women sexy. I got his details and told him I was going to summons him for Soliciting a Prostitute, and he would have to go to court. He started crying and told me he was married with children. This almost broke my heart. Choking back tears I said, 'Stiff shit you sick bastard. You are going to have to tell your wife and kids what you were doing then. Now get out of here before I lock you up.'

As I watched him drive off crying, I could not believe what shit magnets hookers are. They attracted the lowest level scum anyone could imagine. I walked over to Trixie and believe it or not she was freshly zonked. Some other low life had sold and injected her with heroin. The only way she would have got the money for the heroin was if she had already turned a trick before we got there. So some

49

other sick bastard had already been and gone. She could hardly talk and was worse than the first time we picked her up.

I called another ambulance and again waited with her until they arrived. I put my coat over her until they did. When the ambos got there, they put her in the back again and I got my overcoat back. It stunk and she had dribbled this gooey shit all over the front. I handled it like a porcupine and chucked it behind the seat. It was going straight to the dry cleaners the next day and if that did not work, I would chuck it out.

Trixie had her baby that morning. In fact, she started contractions in the ambulance. Her baby was born full term but was soon diagnosed with having a heroin addiction. Apparently, the foetus can become addicted to the heroin whilst in the womb if the mother continues to use during the pregnancy. What chance did that poor little bugger have? What a start to life. I doubt whether mum would still be alive, and I would have serious doubts about the child as well. Some of these scumbags should be neutered so they cannot destroy anyone else's life, especially someone who does not have the choice of mother or addiction.

CHAPTER NINE

Police Versus Mad Dog and Max

I found myself working yet another 7am van shift on another Sunday morning. I thought I must be in the bad books with the roster sergeant, this was about the third Sunday morning shift in a month. I wondered whether it was the boss's way of trying to keep me off the turps.

Saturday was always a big night for everyone at St Kilda. Most of the blokes there were young, single and not on bad coin, so it was a dangerous mix.

Every night became Saturday night after a while and it was very rare that myself and the others on the same shift wouldn't have anywhere from 10 to 100 beers after work. Figuratively speaking of course.

If that meant fronting up at 7am the next morning. So be it.

They didn't breath test coppers at all in those days, or most of the road crews would never have got out of the station. Nearly every copper in uniform and in the CIB would've been in the walker's club, as they'd have done their tickets at least one out of any seven days.

I was working with a copper we will call Laughing Boy as he laughed all the time including sometimes when the reaction should have been anything but a laugh. He had also been out with me the night before. Neither of us remembered exactly what time we'd finished. But it was after midnight and we were a little tired and potentially cranky.

We got to the station and signed out our shooter and went straight out and completed the vehicle inspection check list, as was the regulation when taking out any police vehicle.

We went to the side of the station where the divisional van was parked and Laughing Boy said, 'Is that a van?'

I replied, 'Affirmative.'

'Has it got everything it should have?'

'Affirmative.'

'There, done. Do you want to drive or will I?'

I said, 'I'll drive. You look worse than me.'

That was as thorough as the vehicle check list was ever done. Things were only fixed when they were crashed, broken, flat or buggered, for any of a multitude of reasons. Routine or preventative maintenance had not been invented yet. That was why no smart copper ever bought a second-hand police car.

We might have been crazy, but we weren't stupid. When it came to coppers saving money, most would kill their mothers before wasting a quid.

I chucked my hat in the van and he jumped in the passenger side and picked up the microphone and said, 'VKC this is St Kilda 307 Code 1.'

The D24 operator responded with a bored and nonchalant 'Roger that St Kilda 307'.

Off we went aimlessly driving around the suburb at just after 7am on a Sunday. We were both in low gear and he suggested we head down Fitzroy Street and get something to eat.

The St Kilda Cafe was the only place open at that time of the day and it was a matter of making the most out of what we had available. We needed fat, sugar and salt and the Cafe had all three in spades.

I did a U turn and headed towards the street at a leisurely pace. We got to Fitzroy Street and had travelled about a block doing the crawl.

I came to a stop outside the café and noticed a big tall bastard came out. He was in an extremely excitable state and was bouncing around and yelling obscenities to no one in particular. He didn't seem to have noticed the divvy van stopped just up from him. He was about 6' 4" tall, looked fit as Mallee Bull and built like a brick shithouse. He was dancing around like a professional boxer and his eyes were wide open.

When he yelled it was with such force that the bones and muscles at the front of his neck and chin flexed. He was well dressed and had a couple of tattoos visible on both of his muscular forearms. He was wearing a nice-looking pair of slacks, an in fashion short sleeve shirt that accentuated his build and a good-looking pair of leather dress shoes.

I said, 'Hey, call this dickhead over and we'll see what he's up to.'

It was common practice to call people of interest, usually crooks and hookers, over to the passenger side of the van and they'd be initially questioned to see if there was any reason to suspect they had any drugs or weapons on them. If they tweaked the interest of the van crew, then both coppers would get out, separate and search whoever it was.

He yelled out through his already open window to this bloke, who we later labelled Mad Dog, for reasons that will become obvious shortly. 'Hey mate. Come over here for a second.'

Mad Dog looked straight at him and said, 'Get fucked. You come here.'

He then spread his feet and stood there with his arms crossed and leaned the top half of his body back in a defiant display of bad manners.

'I'll give D24 a location just in case. This bloke's mad as a meat axe. He's got to be on some serious shit,' I said.

With that he opened his door and was walking towards Mad Dog, who was now facing the street with his back against a shop window and smiling at Laughing Boy.

As he was getting out, I picked up the microphone for the police radio that was mounted on the dash of the divvy van. 'VKC this is St Kilda 307 over.'

The D24 operator responded immediately with 'St Kilda 307 go ahead.'

I was just about to give my message when I saw Mad Dog lunge at Laughing Boy and they started wrestling. In the first few seconds I could see we were going to be no match for this bloke and saw him take a big punch to the face that sent him flying backwards onto the ground. Mad Dog pounced on top of him and was trying to punch him in the face again.

I yelled into the microphone, 'St Kilda 307 Urgent. Police in trouble outside the St Kilda Café in Fitzroy Street.'

I threw the microphone on the vacant passenger seat and bolted out of the van to help my mate. As I did so I could hear the D24 operator call, 'Any unit clear near Fitzroy Street, St Kilda? We have police in trouble at that location. Any unit clear.'

I heard a number of units start to reply but then I turned my mind to the crook. As I got around the van Mad Dog was astride Laughing Boy, who was lying on the footpath on his back and was trying to fend off punch after punch to his head and body.

I ran at Mad Dog and just before I was about to blindside him and belt him over the head with my baton, he turned and saw me coming at close range. As quick as a flash, he started to stand and was almost facing me when I hit him right across the front of his head with the baton.

In those days the baton consisted of three strands of pretty thick wire connected to a concrete block at the end. The whole thing was encased in rubber with a leather strap for a wrist grip. The idea was to slip the baton strap over your wrist, so you didn't lose it during a fight.

I didn't have time to wrap the strap as I'd only pulled it out of my baton pocket as I got around the front of the van. Police trousers had a baton pocket sewn into the right-hand leg, so the baton could be held in it and let the strap hang out near the pocket. This was so it could be drawn quickly if needed.

Anyway, I was only holding the baton by the rubber grip and hadn't put the strap around my wrist. I swung hard and hit Mad Dog across the right side of his head.

He didn't even flinch and instead responded with a punch to my jaw that sent me straight to the ground. I landed on my back and Mad Dog dived on top of me and started giving me the same treatment he'd been giving Laughing Boy prior to my attempted rescue. He hit me several times and I hit him a couple of times. I hit him flush on the button but that didn't even slow him down. He was roaring at me and his eyes were wide and glazed and he looked like a real crazy bastard.

I knew I was in all sorts of strife.

While Mad Dog was doing his best to belt the living suitcase out of me, Laughing Boy had started to get a second wind and crash tackled Mad Dog from the side. They toppled off me and he ended up on top of him. I rolled over and got astride Mad Dog as Laughing Boy tried to restrain his arms. We were going as hard as we could but couldn't manage to get his arms close enough to handcuff him.

Realising that my punches weren't affecting him, I thought I'd try and strangle him instead. As Laughing Boy continued to wrestle him, I placed my hands around Mad Dog's throat and was trying to apply what was referred to as 'The Chicken'.

This was designed to strangle the person and render them unconscious, at which time most crooks it was used on would involuntarily move their arms and or legs like a chicken. Thus the name. I was normally very capable when it came to applying the chicken and could execute the hold from the front or the rear of the person trying to be restrained.

Mad Dog was flexing his chest and neck muscles and was proving nearly impossible to subdue or chicken. Then he let out a whistle through his teeth and called out, 'Get him Max.'

My heart nearly fell out of my chest and I thought we were in deep shit now. He's got a friend.

It took a millisecond for that thought to occur to me, when all of a sudden I was attacked from behind. I felt a hard push which knocked me off Mad Dog and onto all fours on the footpath alongside him and Laughing Boy, who were still going at it.

I felt a set of teeth latch onto my right shoulder and the fetid stink of someone's breath near my right ear. I felt something thrusting at my bottom, causing me to instinctively clench the cheeks of my arse as hard as I could.

I thought for one terrifying second, 'Don't tell me I am going to be rooted as well as beaten to death?'

I reached my arm up and felt the fur of a dog's head trying to bite through the shoulder of my police tunic. I later thanked my lucky stars I'd worn my tunic that day, instead of just my thin police issue uniform shirt.

While I was preoccupied with the dog, his owner had landed several punches to Laughing Boy's head and body and had managed to get away from him.

He started jogging backwards away from the scene of the fight. My offsider lay on the footpath moaning and bleeding before he managed to gather some reserve of energy and got up and kicked the dog in the guts. The dog yelped but didn't let go or stop trying to tear my shoulder apart with his powerful jaws.

As Mad Dog pranced backwards down the middle of Fitzroy Street, he whistled again and thankfully Max let go of my shoulder. I rolled onto my back to see a large German Shepherd running away from me towards his master.

Laughing Boy got himself together and with baton drawn ran off after him as best he could, though he looked to be favouring his right side and was obviously in pain.

Mad Dog was yelling at us, 'Come on you weak dogs. Come and get me.'

I tried to get to my feet and felt a knife-like pain in my ribs and recognised the thick salty taste of my own blood in my mouth. I quickly felt around with my tongue to survey the damage and could feel the jagged edges of at least two broken teeth.

I looked at Laughing Boy running up and down and looking like something out of the Keystone Cops, with his baton waving in the air while the crook easily avoided each charge like some sort of toreador.

He was making us look like dickheads and that pissed me off just as much as getting the crap belted out of me.

I yelled to come back and we'll get him with the van. He stopped his pursuit and gingerly jogged back to the divvy van. I asked him to drive because I didn't think I could. He jumped in the van and cranked it up. He jammed it in gear and let out the clutch shooting us straight for where Mad Dog was prancing around in the middle of the street on the tram tracks.

When he saw the van coming at him, he ran to the western side of the street, on the opposite side to the café. I could hear the radio alive with chatter and heard a unit say they were going to be in Fitzroy Street in a minute or so. I thought I could hear the siren but thought that might just be wishful thinking and put my mind back to the task at hand.

He ran onto the footpath and was running now at full pelt trying to get past the point of convergence with where our van was heading. He aimed the van right at him and he jumped over a small brick fence bordering the footpath and into someone's front yard.

He was obviously in pain and wasn't at his best behind the wheel. He didn't hit the brakes soon enough and next thing we knew we'd crashed the van into the fence and came to rest inside the front yard. He jammed the van into reverse and backed out of the yard. I could hear the knocking of bricks against the undercarriage and sides of the van but didn't really give a rat's arse. All we were concerned about was catching this crazy bastard and locking him up.

He reversed and was straightening up on the roadway when we heard a new screaming siren as another marked police van flew around a nearby corner. Thank God for that. The cavalry was here and not too soon either. He pointed at Mad Dog who was running away south towards the beach still in the middle of the road. The other van took off after him and came to a sudden stop right in front of him, blocking his path.

We ascertained the damage was a flat tyre and two bent wheels, not to mention the body damage from going through the brick fence.

We pulled up next to the other van, whose flashing lights and siren were still wailing. We jumped out and between the four of us managed to catch and pin the mad bastard to the ground. He still put up a fight and the two new constables in the melee didn't get out unscathed either.

Mad Dog took more punishment from the four of us than I'd seen anyone take and still he fought on. He was obviously on some serious shit and they kept him going when a normal man would've given up or been pinned long ago.

We finally got the cuffs on him and we had to continue to wrestle him into the back of the other van. Another couple of police cars arrived at the same time and they, more than us, managed to get him into the back of the van.

Before they had a chance to close and padlock the rear door of the divvy van, along came Max. In all the excitement we had clean forgotten about Max and weren't impressed as we saw the dog run past and jump into the back of the van.

The crook was laughing at us and calling us 'fucking pigs, fucking maggots, fucking dogs' in a continuous tirade of vitriol, interspersed with mouthfuls of saliva mixed with blood that he was spitting at all police present.

When Max jumped in one of the other coppers said to no one in particular, 'What do you want to do about the dog?'

Laughing Boy said, 'Bugger the dog. Leave it there. I just want to get this crazy bastard back to the office. We can work out the dog then'.

The whole posse of police vans and cars then drove back to the police station.

We had to hitch a ride in one of the nearby station sedans and a trainee constable was left with our damaged van.

When we got back to the station we had to wait until someone got a dog handler to subdue and restrain Max before we could get his master out. We moved between the back of the van and the watch house assessing our most serious injuries but were still full of adrenalin and never thought of not seeing this through to the end.

Mad Dog was finally dragged out of the van still kicking and fighting even with his hands cuffed behind his back. His clothing was smeared with blood. Unfortunately, most of it belonged to us.

He was wrestled to an interview room and left handcuffed to a desk while we briefed the sergeant and another Senior Constable. The senior was well built and probably the best-looking bloke you'd see. Girls went weak at the knees when he flashed his perfect teeth at them and everything about him was what I would call military in bearing. He looked like he had been fitted personally for his uniform and had been buffed and ironed into it.

We all went back into the interview room and the sergeant said, 'Listen mate. Settle down and we'll take the cuffs off you. But if you start up again, more people are going to get hurt. Do you understand?'

Mad Dog had seemed to have settled down and appeared to be tired out. His head was bowed and his muscled shoulders were slumped as far as the handcuffs would allow. It appeared to be the tired slump of surrender. Or a very clever ruse to suck the coppers in and have one more go!

The two coppers moved over to him and took the two sets of cuffs off him.

No sooner had they unshackled him than he pushed off from his seat and head butted the senior right in the face. The force of the blow pushed him backwards across a desk. He then set upon the sergeant and was trading blows in between wrestling with him.

We were standing outside in the hallway with the door open and had warned the sergeant this bloke was on something and was as strong as buggery.

Laughing Boy had picked up his baton and held it in his hand behind his back while the negotiation was going on. When I asked what he was doing, he told me his hands were so sore he couldn't punch the prick again if he sparks up and I couldn't help but agree with the sentiment.

Once the fresh action started, I rushed into the room and joined in the fight. The sergeant was doing most of the work as I was knackered and was running on empty.

All of a sudden, I heard someone yell, 'Duck'. At that time I was standing to the right of crazy boy and the sergeant was more to the left side. I ducked and turned my head towards the voice, in time to see the Senior Connie swing his baton full pelt at Mad Dog.

In a superhuman show of strength, he unbelievably managed to shove the sergeant around in front of him and he copped the full force in his upper arm. He let out a yell and was knocked sideways across a table and onto a typewriter before falling to the ground.

By this time every copper in the station had heard the yelling and screaming and came rushing into the interview room. I don't remember how many it took to finally get him into a position to handcuff him, but it was at least six.

When everything had settled down, I was sitting on the floor in the interview room with my back to the wall in a shitload of pain from my broken teeth, ribs and my right hand had swollen up like a balloon.

The sergeant was hanging shit on the Senior Connie for belting him in the arm and was showing anyone who asked, and some who didn't, the bruise on his arm.

Laughing Boy was sitting in an office chair bent over and holding his head in his hands. He had blood all over his face, hands and his uniform was wrecked, as was mine.

Mad Dog lay on the floor with two coppers sitting on him to keep him down.

The Police Doctor had been called and arrived a short time later. An ambulance was also called by the watch house keeper and they arrived before the police doctor. When the ambulance officers were escorted into the interview room, they stood there trying to take in the scene of absolute carnage and destruction. Not to mention the condition of Laughing Boy, myself and to a much lesser extent the crook.

One of the ambos said, 'Bloody hell. What's this? The OK Corral.'

We briefed them and they could see for themselves there was no way the nutter was going to calm down. They ended up giving him some form of sedative that finally stopped him fighting, kicking out and trying to kill everyone. They reckon they gave him so much more of the drug than they normally used on someone gone off his nut and couldn't believe the fight in the bloke.

We ended up in the hospital and were treated for our injuries.

Laughing Boy had two broken ribs, concussion, numerous cuts and abrasions, a broken right hand and a broken big toe, apparently from when he kicked the dog.

I had to have a dentist attend the hospital and do enough dental work on the two broken teeth to stop the exposed nerves from driving me insane. I also had two broken ribs on one side and one broken rib on the other. I had a badly broken right hand and one of my knuckles was pushed back into the hand and was badly broken. We both had two black eyes each, but my offsider was lucky his nose was alright, while mine was broken.

Over the next couple of days the bruising was well and truly at its peak and we looked like we'd been hit by a truck. I've never forgotten Mad Dog and Max. I still think it was the worst hiding I'd had.

Mad Dog was charged with numerous counts of Assault Police and Assault Causing Serious Injury. I know he did time but I don't remember how long a stretch he got. We never saw him again thank goodness.

Perception is a marvellous thing and I've had various opinions as to how funny this event was. Even though we got the crap belted out of us, I still think it's a funny story.

CHAPTER TEN

Donald Hatherley Tries to Shoot Me

While I was stationed at the St Kilda Police Station, I was performing Special Duties with two of the best blokes I've ever worked with. The Sergeant was a dual Valour Award Winner and one of the funniest blokes I've ever met, Paul Mullet. The other was Senior Constable Vasilios Panagiotaros aka Bill Smith, or simply The Wog. Obviously political correctness hadn't been invented yet. We were on Special Duties for six months and I used this time as my launching pad for my CIB Board. The idea was to take up as many offenders for as many offences as I could, to show my ability and capacity to work hard and for extended periods.

We had a ball doing Specials, as it was referred to, and had many a crazy shift with the highly amusing Sergeant Mullet and The Wog.

We managed to arrest around one hundred offenders for almost seven hundred offences. One of the ones we didn't charge was one of the ones that nearly cost me my life. The crook's name was Donald George Hatherley. A violent and demented rapist and sex offender.

On this particular day in early 1986, Billy and I were working when we were called by Senior Detective from the St Kilda CIB. Apparently he had a victim for a violent rape and had a suspect in a vehicle that he wanted us to sit off while he took the complainant's statement and sorted out exactly what had happened.

Bill and I took off in the unmarked police car we used for Specials and I can't remember how but we ended up tailing the offender in his vehicle. It was either a panel van or a ute and it had a bench seat in the front. The reason I remember the bench seat so vividly will become obvious very shortly.

We followed this scumbag through St Kilda and our instructions were to prop him if he tried to leave the St Kilda area.

After following him around for a while, he turned left into Hotham Street heading towards Princes Highway, which was the geographical boundary between St Kilda and Prahran's area. Hotham Street was and still is a two-lane carriageway, as the police parlance goes, and the east side is boarded by the St Kilda Cemetery.

It was about four in the afternoon and the traffic was reasonable, without being heavy. I hated trying to follow anyone, as I reckoned it was a bastard of a job and found it extremely hard to stay with the target without becoming obvious. Anyway, we managed to keep up with him somehow without him being any the wiser.

As he stopped in the line of traffic in Hotham Street just south of Princes Highway we decided to pounce and arrest this dirt bag before he cleared St Kilda.

We'd alerted D24 as to what we were planning and asked for the St Kilda divvy van to assist with the intercept, while the suspect was still in his car stuck in traffic.

We had no idea whether he was armed or not and had no reason to suspect he carried weapons, as we really didn't know much about him at that time.

Our divvy van with two constables came down Hotham Street heading south as we pulled over facing north and approached the crook's car. I went to the front driver's side of the car and held

my police ID (or Freddie) out in front of me and yelled for the
driver to get out of the car with his hands up. I had my revolver
drawn and had it by my side but wasn't pointing it at Hatherley
at that stage.

Billy Panagiotaros was doing likewise on the passenger side and
it probably looked very dramatic to the other drivers sitting in the
traffic in front and around the crook's car.

Hatherley looked straight at me and let go with the clutch and
the car jumped forward. I tried to jump out of the way but I wasn't
fast enough. He hit my leg with the front of his car and knocked
me flying onto the roadway.

Then he slammed the gears into reverse, hitting the car behind
him, before again changing gears and driving straight at me as I was
scrambling to my feet. I managed to get out of the way this time
and his vehicle bounced off the car in front of him and rolled back
a few feet. I continued yelling at this prick to get out of the car. By
now I was pointing my pistol at him as I yelled out to him.

Just as this happened, one of the uniform coppers approached the
crook's ute from the front driver's side and pulled the door open.

The knucklehead very nearly got him and at least one of us killed.

He approached the car just in front of me and stuck his revolver
through the open door. Hatherley leaned back from the window,
as I suppose I would've done too. Then he took hold of the pistol
which was still attached to the constable and dragged it into the car.

To the coppers credit he kept hold of the revolver and followed
it in through the open door and ended up on top of Hatherley as
they struggled with the gun.

I was yelling at the copper to get the bloody gun out and he
yelled back he couldn't. It would've looked quite comical at this
stage because there was Bill and I yelling and then ducking every
time the gun was pointed in our direction. I was shitting myself

and had grave concerns for the Connie and the rest of us as this struggle continued.

I ran at the door and after trying to wrestle the two apart, whilst keeping a close eye on the location of the revolver, I ended up three deep across the bench seat with the crook on the bottom facing upwards, the uniform copper was lying on top of him facing downwards and I was on top of him also facing Hatherley. Everyone was yelling and the gun continued to be pointed in all directions, with the battle to control the trigger the primary objective.

I leaned up on my right arm across the copper's back and was punching Hatherley in the head with my left hand. As I was reliant on my right hand, I was landing punches, but they lacked the power of my right hand, which I couldn't manage to bring into the fray.

Then Hatherley yelled like a stuck pig and reefed the pistol out of the copper's hand and it ended up in his.

All this happened very quickly and the next thing I knew was I could feel something hard and round being pushed into the ribs under my right arm. No it wasn't because he was happy to see me!

I looked around and saw it was the revolver being stuck into my ribs and for some unknown reason I looked straight into Hatherley's face. I remember looking into his eyes for that split second and I swear the bastard was smiling at me. If I ever imagined looking into the face of evil this was it. It was a look of manic malevolence. He looked like he wanted to kill me and he looked like he was going to enjoy it immensely. This galvanised me into action rather than cause me to panic and pause. At least from then on I knew I could handle a dangerous situation and not freeze. I didn't get time to fully appreciate this talent as I fought to survive the present situation.

As I looked at him, I rolled onto my left side, freeing up my right arm and took hold of the gun. I remembered at the academy being shown how to jam the web part of your hand between the thumb and the pointer finger into the spot where the hammer falls back onto to cause the gun to fire. I couldn't believe I remembered it when I had to.

As I jammed my hand between the hammer and the block, I could see him with his finger on the trigger and he couldn't understand why the gun wasn't firing.

Although this proved very effective, it hurt like a bitch and I was shaking the weapon around trying to get my hand out. This was an instinctive reaction to pain, and I have no doubt I should not have been trying to get my hand out as that would enable the weapon to fire. I ended up pushing the weapon away from my ribs but in doing so, my hand's webbing came clear of the hammer and I really thought I was cactus at that stage.

I pushed the gun away from me towards the floor just as I heard a deafening bang and realised the prick had fired the pistol. I didn't think at that stage that he'd tried to shoot me and that didn't quite dawn on me until it was all over.

When I heard the shot fired, I grabbed hold of the gun with both hands by sliding around almost onto my back on top of the Connie, who was still sandwiched between the two of us. I can't remember what he was doing but I think he was trying to punch the crook as all this was going on.

When I got two hands on the gun and kept it pointed at the ground, Billy had managed to open the passenger side door by smashing the window and he grabbed hold of the bastard and joined in.

It takes a lot of guts to do what Billy did that day, especially when there's a loaded firearm being pointed at him intermittently as he tried to get into the cabin.

When the shot was fired it would've been quite understandable if he'd backed off.

He didn't and he smashed the window and saved our arses. We managed to overpower Hatherley and Bill pulled him out of the car through the passenger door, before pinning him to the ground and handcuffing him.

I tried to assist as best I could, but it was then I started to realise how close I'd come to being dead.

I remember Bill looking at me when he had the crook trussed up like a prize pig. He had a look of fear on his face. It wasn't so much fear for himself, but I could tell he was more fearful for my safety. At that stage, I got out of the car and I remember Bill said to me, 'Did he hit you?'

I remember thinking to myself, 'Of course he hit me. We were trading punches the whole time we were in there.'

Then it dawned on me. He'd fired a shot in the car. Fuck. Have I been hit? Have I been hit by a bloody bullet?

I stood on the footpath and was running my hands over my chest and my sides like I was trying to find a bee hidden in my clothing. I turned around and showed Bill my back to get him to check and see if there were any holes there.

Bill performed a thorough examination and said, 'No. Can't see anything. Shit how lucky was that?'

I walked over to a fence off the footpath and all of a sudden my legs felt like lead and I was absolutely knackered. I fell more than sat on the fence and fumbled around, first finding my gun in its holster and then searching myself for my smokes.

I took one out of the packet with shaky hands and tried to light it, which I couldn't. I can't remember who lit it for me but someone did and I sat there shaking my head realising how close to moving to the other side of the cemetery wall I'd come.

Then I heard a loud voice saying something in a very excited manner. I looked up as the Connie walked towards me with a smile on his face and was saying, 'How good was that? Shit that was unbelievable.'

He had this stupid look on his face and all I wanted to do was punch him right on the dial. I jumped up from the fence and moved towards him throwing my smoke to the ground and yelling through gritted teeth and a nasty looking snarl, 'Exciting? You fucking idiot! You nearly got us killed. I'll give you exciting you dickhead!'

I'd lost the plot and was hell bent on belting the deadshit.

That wasn't allowed to happen, and I can't remember who stopped it but someone intervened. Afterwards he wasn't smiling and he was definitely not mouthing off how exciting he thought the whole incident was.

Hatherley was taken back to St Kilda CIB and was interviewed and charged with Aggravated Rape, a variety of assaults on the rape victim and us, Resisting Arrest and Using a Firearm to Prevent Apprehension. The scumbag was interviewed and charged by the CIB detectives and they got the conviction.

Just to prove there must be a god, Hatherley was killed in prison by a rather nasty dementor by the name of Paul Steven Haig.

Haig was at that stage in the state's history, one of the worst serial killers to ever breathe our air. He'd murdered six people and was in prison when he assisted Donald Hatherley to kill himself.

Whether he assisted him or just killed him will never be known.

Haig had killed two people in separate hold-ups in 1978 and stated, 'They threatened my freedom and the last thought I had before I pulled the trigger was "You're not sending me back to jail".'

Then in 1979 he committed an atrocity that even hardened crooks would never condone. He killed Sheryl Gardner, a

31-year-old mother in front of her 10-year-old son. After consoling the boy for a short time, he fired three shots into his head killing him instantly.

As if that wasn't depraved and sick enough, his next victim was his 19-year-old girlfriend Lisa Brearley. He stabbed her more than 150 times. He told police during the interview that he was obsessed about the number of times he stabbed her, but he kept losing score and would have to start again. When her front had no room left for more stab wounds he turned her body over and continued stabbing her in the back. He stated he only stopped stabbing her when he was satisfied there was no chance of a 'miraculous recovery'.

Haigh would later tell the Supreme Court, in January 2008 when he was applying to have a minimum term set for his seven murders, that he was remorseful about all the murders except that of Hatherley. He detailed how he 'assisted' him to suicide while they were in jail together in 1991. He even told the court it was done with consent and that it was something that was done with warmth.

Yeah right. This bloke was obviously one sick puppy and hopefully he'll never experience freedom in this lifetime.

In a surprising twist it turned out that Peter Spence, my future boss at the Major Crime Squad, spent two years on a task force hunting Haig before he was caught and jailed. So the five degrees of separation comes to the fore again. Good riddance to Donald George Hatherley.

CHAPTER ELEVEN

Escape of the Dead Man

This was yet another 7am shift on a Sunday morning for me and once again I am sure I was the innocent victim of a drink spiking the night before. Someone must've tampered with one of the 124 beers I'd had. I was feeling less than at my peak and should've known my reputation as a shit magnet would be further enhanced. I was working with another constable who was known as Chip as there were two coppers stationed at St Kilda with the same name and he was the younger. So chip off the old block became Chip. He was a good-looking younger bloke who stood about 6' 1" and was pretty well built. He loved a beer and was an absolute hoot to work with, as you'd never know what he was going to say or do.

Chip and I were rostered to work the divvy van which consisted of driving around aimlessly hanging shit on anyone we thought looked different or strange, of which there was definitely no shortage in St Kilda. This was also referred to by some police as patrolling.

Anyway, we hit the road at 7am and got a job straight away. We were told to attend to a possible dead body in a block of flats in one of the side streets off Fitzroy Street. I remember looking at him and saying, 'Shit. You have got to be shitting me. Seven am on a fucking Sunday morning and we get a body.'

He didn't say much as he'd been with me the night before and was also feeling a little tired and emotional.

We pulled the divvy van up out the front of a block of flats that consisted of three levels each side of a common stairwell. The building was made of brick as was everything in those days and the block had a small front lawn with a row of rose bushes at the front of the building that ran from each side of the footpath approach. It was reasonably well presented and that made me a little happier, as I hated going to the usual drug shithouses where dirty druggies normally frequented and overdosed.

Of course the flat we had to attend was on the third and top floor of the block on the right side of the centre stairwell. We both laboured our way up the steps with Chip whinging that he hadn't even had breakfast yet and he was hungry and thirsty. I grumpily looked at him and said, 'Will you shut the fuck up. I haven't had anything to eat or drink since my last hundred beers at some stage yesterday and I don't feel like walking up these fucking stairs either. We'll just knock this over quick and get back to the office and do the paperwork and we can get something then.'

He complied and was used to my sometimes-gruff demeanour and thought I was hilarious whether I was trying to be happy or sad. I could be the most contrary, obnoxious, vitriolic and negative prick when I wanted to be. I could also be the exact opposite and enjoyed cracking jokes and making fun out of some ordinary tasks. The latter was usually at the expense of someone else which made it even funnier to him. I could say the most outrageous bullshit to members of the public, other coppers, crooks or anyone else for that matter and say it with a straight face. I'd appear to be very sombre and a complete professional when I was actually taking the piss out of them or putting them up for public ridicule without them knowing.

It sounds terrible but the dark humour was a big hit with coppers in those days. In fact, when I saw the movie *Super Troopers*, I nearly died laughing at some of the stupid shit they did in the movie and remembering some of the moronic and hilarious shit we got up to at times. Luckily, my mother, father and sisters didn't hear our coarse language, which was how we spoke. We were young blokes full of piss and sometimes bad manners and this was used to enhance the dark humour. We didn't use that language around women, children or nice people. We saved it to add emphasis to what we were discussing and to enable the druggies to understand us. This was the druggies and the crook's language and we plumbed their depths for dramatic effect to start with. It stuck and became a constant part of our dark vernacular.

Anyway, we lumbered to the top of the stairs and checked the numbers. There was one flat on each side and the one we were looking for was on the right. I noticed the door was wide open and looked at Chip with a 'what's going on here' look. I walked to the door and called out, 'Hello. It's the police, is anyone home?'

There was no response and I knocked a little louder and repeated my call to the occupant. There was still no response, so I walked into the flat and went to the right while making a hand signal to check out the left. I walked straight into the one and only bedroom which was situated at the front of the flat with a view over the front yard to the street. There was a large figure in the bed on the left side with the blankets pulled up to his neck and he appeared to be sound asleep.

I approached and gave the bloke a nudge on the shoulder and said, 'Hey mate. Are you OK?'

There was no movement or acknowledgement. I did this like I was trying to wake my own father and took great pains to be respectful and not frighten buggery out of the bloke in case he was simply asleep.

Chip returned to the room from having checked out the rest of the flat. He told me it was clear and that there was no one else home. I gave the bloke in the bed another nudge and repeated my enquiry as to his health. There was still no movement or response. I pulled the covers back far enough to see the occupant of the bed was a man probably in his late 70s or early 80s with a classic comb over which was all over the place.

He was a fair size old bloke and would have hit the scales around the 100kg mark. He was a nice-looking elderly gentleman and had obviously been well looked after by someone. I felt for a pulse and after a short time turned to Chip and told him it looked like the poor bloke was dead.

Chip, obviously without thinking too hard, asked me if I thought the old bloke had called D24. I looked at him and replied with a laugh, 'God, you are a bloody numbskull. How do you reckon he would've called anyone when he's dead? You say some stupid shit sometimes.'

He laughed and was in no way offended, but rather enjoyed the banter.

He replied, 'Well smart arse, what are we going to do now?'

I told him to get onto D24 and see who called the job in and tell them there's one elderly male and we're trying to locate next of kin and we'll get back to them. He tried using the portable police radio which of course didn't work and so he had to go back down the stairs to use the radio in the van. I had a look around the flat. It was a little place with a master bedroom, living room with a TV in the corner, a small bathroom and a small kitchen. I was trying to locate any next of kin to contact but it kept gnawing at me that the door was open when we got there and yet there was no one around.

There were no signs of a struggle and no obvious injuries to the deceased, other than he wasn't breathing. He came back up the stairs and told me he'd spoken to D24 and that the report had been made by a Mrs X of that address, who was an older lady. He said D24 were organising undertakers, but it could be an hour or two before they got there. He told me the body would be taken to the morgue by the undertakers anyway, so there was no need to get a doctor there.

'What do we do now? Stuck here for an hour or two with a dead body and I'm starving,' he said.

I called him a whinging bastard and suggested he turn on the little telly and see what was on. He turned it on and apart from a test pattern on one channel there was the start of a soccer match from England on the other channel. We weren't impressed. I suggested he go back to the van and head to the St Kilda Cafe and get us some breakfast, in the hope that something to eat and drink would stop his whinging. He wasn't overly impressed about having to take on the stairs again and go to all the trouble of going and getting the sustenance we needed to revive our flagging spirits. I managed to sweet talk him and he agreed to go and leave me at the flat. I gave him some cash and off he went while I took up a position on the couch and sat there quietly contemplating just how crook I felt and how tired I was.

I must have closed my eyes and was sound asleep when I heard the door opening and Chip yelling out, 'Darling, I'm home.' I woke and sat bolt upright before laughing at the idiot. I thought to myself what a dick he would've looked if I'd managed to track down any next of kin. He would have walked in with his 'Darling I'm home'.

He carried a white plastic bag containing some form of sumptuous fare that was to be our breakfast. He unpacked it on the table and I was most impressed with the good work he'd done. Breakfast consisted of a hamburger with the lot in a white paper bag, two fried dim sums, two potato cakes and a cold can of Coke for each of us. I knew there was enough fat, grease, sugar and salt in this meal to cure anything, but more particularly the alcohol induced lethargy we were both suffering. Hedge turned on the TV and sat on the couch next to me and we hooked into our hearty feast whilst enjoying the soccer, which neither of us knew the rules to or understood in any way.

Halfway through our breakfast with us both lounging on our respective halves of the couch, the front door opened and in walked a well-dressed lady in her 70s carrying shopping bags. We jumped to our feet and tried to finish the mouthful of food that was rendering us both incommunicado. When this was achieved, I approached the kitchen bench and watched as the lady began putting the shopping away and it struck me as strange that she hadn't acknowledged our presence or said anything.

I asked the lady if she was Mrs X and she said she was and continued putting the shopping away. I was speaking in a regulated tone and trying to come across as polite and professional as I could in the circumstances.

I said, 'Mrs X, I'm Constable Joe Noonan from the St Kilda Police Station. Is that your husband in the bedroom?'

She spoke in what I would describe as a robotic manner and was very matter of fact. She kept putting away the groceries and answered, 'Yes that my husband. Is he still asleep?'

'I'm sorry to inform you that your husband has passed away,' I said.

'He has not passed away thank you very much constable. He is asleep,' she replied.

I knew she was in shock and asked the lady to come with me and escorted her into the bedroom. I lifted the covers back enough to show the face of her husband and said, 'Is this your husband Mrs X?'

She said it was and again stated he wasn't dead but asleep. After finally convincing her he was in fact deceased, I took the lady back into the lounge room. It still gets me why we avoided the use of the word dead and always used deceased. I'm not sure whether it was that dead sounded harsh or maybe we all said deceased to make ourselves sound clever.

By this stage Chip had cleaned up all the food wrappers and cans. I asked Mrs X to find any relatives' details so I could notify them. I began calling people out of a personal phone book she had in her handbag. I made the calls. It was never a pleasant task to deal with death notifications, nor was it pleasant to sit with this poor woman who was struggling to accept the fact that her husband of many decades was gone forever.

Within half an hour relatives began arriving and although distressed were able to provide comfort to Mrs X. I remembered there were a couple of nieces and at least one of her sisters. After another hour or more had elapsed the undertakers finally arrived in their van and parked out the front. I met them and explained the circumstances and forewarned them there were relatives in the flat, so watch their language and be very respectful how they handled the body.

They looked like Laurel and Hardy. One was a big barrel-chested bloke with a huge beer gut and thick dark hair on his large boof head. The other was shorter, skinny and obviously played second fiddle to the bigger bloke.

The big bloke must have weighed in at over 140kg and was sweating heavily from his forehead. It was running down his face on both sides. He looked like someone who'd just finished a run rather than someone who'd just got his fat arse out of a funeral van.

I nicknamed the undertakers Fatso and Arnie to Chip, who loved every smart arse comment I made about this less than dynamic duo. Fatso was pretty obvious and Arnie was a short reference to Arnold Schwarzenegger, who was in build the exact opposite to this little bloke.

They got to the bottom of the stairwell and Fatso said, 'Don't tell me. He's on the fucking top floor.' I laughed and replied, 'Of course. No one dies on the ground floor, do they?'

They had their stretcher with them with the body bag and straps sitting on top. Fatso led the way with Arni, Chipper and I bringing up the rear, so to speak. It seemed to take an eternity for Fatso to lead the team to the third floor. He regularly had to pause and stand with one leg on the next higher step with all his weight resting on his one arm which in turn was resting on the higher thigh. He was panting and sweating with his shirt all wet under his arms and it was spreading down his back. I kept poking Chip in the arse to make him turn around. When he did he saw me laughing as quietly as I could. I was red as a beetroot at poor old Fatso.

We reached the top eventually and I asked Fatso if he wanted me to call or ambulance. He looked at me and said in gasps, 'Yeah, very fucking funny. Let's just get this over with so I can get the fuck out of here.'

After he got his breath back, I introduced them to Mrs X and escorted them into the bedroom to view the body. I asked Mrs X and the others to stay in the lounge or kitchen so the undertakers could prepare Mr X to move him downstairs. I was very professional and showed a great degree of empathy for the family and they appreciated it.

After half an hour Arnie came out of the flat and told me that they were ready to move the body down the stairs and asked if one of us could help, as the deceased was a fair-sized bloke. I asked how they were going to do it and Arnie went on to explain that they'd strap the body in the body bag onto the stretcher and bring him down the stairs. At each landing which was halfway between levels there was a large window and each of these looked out over the front yard and the street. He said he wanted the windows opened and explained that it was bloody hard manipulating the stretcher with the body on it. Each time they came to the landing they had to turn the body on the stretcher, and he didn't want one of the legs of the stretcher smashing the window as they lifted one end higher and turned it round the corner. I thought it sounded reasonable and after some more discussion it was decided Hedge would help them with the stretcher while I took the relatives out the front of the flat so they weren't there while he was brought out.

I walked out the front and began talking to one of the nieces and was letting them know what would happen from then on. Unbeknown to me, Fatso had one end of the stretcher while Chip and Arnie had the other end. They managed to carry the stretcher out of the tight bedroom and into the hallway. Fatso said to Arnie, 'Listen, you take the other end because I'm going to have to lift the top when we get to each landing and you won't be able to.'

Arnie agreed and took one side of the stretcher while Chip took the other side and they led down the stairs. At the first stairwell landing, they were having trouble turning the stretcher around the U bend. After some time, Fatso said to Arnie, 'Listen, stand off to the side and let Chip stand off to the other side. Put your end of the stretcher lower and I'll raise mine as high as I can and try that.'

As they did this I was continuing on with my small talk out the front not knowing the struggle that was taking place with the body

on the landing between the third and second floor. Back inside
Arnie and Hedge lowered their end of the stretcher and Fatso
heaved and lifted his as high as he could.

Just as he did this, the zipped up green body bag came free and
slid off the end of the stretcher. The strap hadn't been secured
firmly enough holding the body bag to the stretcher and the
bag slid off. Of course, it didn't hit the wall or the side of the
windowsill and fall onto the concrete landing, as distasteful as that
would've been.

No. The body bag came flying out of the second-floor
window closely followed by a loud scream of 'Fuck' from inside
the building.

The body bag fell from the window and landed on an angle,
right in the centre of the mature rose bushes at the front of the
building abutting the wall. These rose bushes were more than
mature. They were bushes and had bloody big branches and thorns
like a brickies thumb. As the thin plastic body bag caught on the
top of the bush, the bag ripped open and the body was then clearly
visible half in and half out of the bag.

The poor bloke's arm had come out of the bag, as had the top
of his body and was hanging off the thorn bushes. Just as this
happened, I looked up and saw Arnie looking out the window,
then Chip and finally a most distraught and exhausted Fatso.

Chip looked out at me and yelled, 'Did you fucking see that?'

I looked at the niece and the rest of the family who looked like
they'd just seen Linda Blair's head going around in circles like in
The Exorcist. They all screamed and stepped back away from their
dead relative.

I was looking at Chip and the two undertakers peering out of
the window. I jammed my mouth shut and had one of the worst
Monty Python moments of my life. I was bright red with tears

streaming down my face whilst nearly suffering an embolism of suppressed laughter that I knew would end my career if it escaped.

I managed to run into the stairwell and up the stairs as fast as I could before I exploded with the most racking unstoppable laughter I'd ever experienced. Chip was also in hysterics and we were both trying to quieten each other which only served to make it worse. Fatso looked like someone had just stolen his last doughnut and Arnie had eyes like golf balls that were about to pop out of his head.

I managed to get myself under some form of control while the undertakers scrambled down and recovered the body as gracefully as they could from the rose bushes. I held it together long enough to comfort the relatives yet again.

I did such a good job that the niece rang our sergeant and expressed her gratitude and even made mention of how Constable Noonan had been so upset by what the undertakers did that he had tears flowing down his face and had to run inside the building to hide his emotion.

This is another example of how the best-intentioned plan can so easily be unravelled, and we could've looked very ordinary indeed that morning. Thank God it worked out for the best and the family were able to get over it and accepted the difficulties the undertakers had in trying to get their uncle down the stairs from the third floor.

I can't understand what would attract anyone to that line of work and often wondered whether they were all there to do such a job. When I think about it, they probably would've said the same about us after some of the things we had to roll up to during our stint at St Kilda and elsewhere in my time in the job.

CHAPTER TWELVE

The Overdose

I was rostered to work the afternoon shift van and kicked off at 3pm. I was working with a big senior constable we'll call Redneck. This was his nickname because he was about 6' 3" and a very solid bloke who'd recently transferred to St Kilda from rural Victoria somewhere. He ambled around like he should've been wearing loose fitting bib and brace overalls with bare feet like someone out of Kissing Cousins in the Missouri backwaters.

He had one of the deepest baritone voices you'd ever hear and spoke a little slower than most of the others. Before he spoke, he always seemed to consider what he was going to say. He was the exact opposite of me in that respect, as I was quick off the mark being a smart arse most of the time.

We loaded all our gear in the divvy van which consisted mainly of our smokes, hats and long black torches that were sometimes used as batons if the need arose. Redneck drove and started patrolling our patch, as the area of responsibility was referred to. He was laughing about the session we'd enjoyed the night before at one of the local pubs. It turned into a huge drink but he loved a drink and was in no way feeling any ill effects from it. I was also in my prime and was feeling good.

About an hour into our shift, we received a call to attend to a laundromat in the main street. The operator passed on there was a report of an unconscious man in the shop. I answered the call with 'St Kilda 311 received. We are about 30 seconds off. Over.'

He gunned the van and headed straight for the laundry mat. He pulled up right outside the shop with a small skid announcing our arrival. We quickly jumped out and walked into the shop. We were greeted halfway in by a very excited looking middle-aged man in his mid to late forties. He was wearing a pair of crappy looking over sized shorts with no belt, which explained why the whole time we were there he was pulling them up or exposing his arse with a disgustingly hairy butt crack. He had on a sweat stained singlet that at one stage of its existence may have been white. It was summer, so he accessorised with a pair of ordinary looking thongs. He was fat as a chocolate taster and was sweating like a pig. What little hair he had left was stuck to his head with some form of lard or hair cream and he had numerous tatts all over his arms and rather chunky legs. He gave off a certain fragrance that was very hard to stand in the presence of without wanting to throw up. Although he looked like Rocky Balboa's brother-in-law, he was from then on referred to as Fabio. This was due mostly to his svelte build, devilish good looks and his obvious dress smarts.

He addressed Redneck as we entered the shop. This was a phenomenon that happened a lot. People always seemed to want to speak to the taller or the more senior of the coppers rolling up to a job. It must have made them feel safer or better for some unknown reason. In this instance, I was grateful I was shorter and younger than my partner.

Fabio pointed at a young scrote about 20 years of age slumped over in a chair opposite the washing and drying machines. The machines were against the side wall and the shop had a glass frontage with chairs along the inside facing into the belly of the shop. The counter was about four metres in from the door and there was a naked concrete slab floor.

Fabio said, 'Can you get this shithead out of here. I don't want dirty fuckers like him dying in the shop.'

Redneck replied quick as flash with, 'Why? What sort of dirty fuckers would you prefer to have die in your shop?'

I kept a straight face as did he.

'What's the story?' he said.

He spoke as we walked over to the young bloke and I felt for a pulse. The patient was about 20 years old, tall and skinny, wearing a pair of filthy denim jeans with no belt. He wore no shoes and had a filthy T-shirt under an aged Hawaiian shirt which was unbuttoned and wide open. He was slumped in the chair with his head leaning on what would have been a most uncomfortable angle, if he'd been conscious at the time, which he most definitely wasn't.

Fabio said, 'If he's dead can you take him out of the shop? I don't want fucking dead druggies in here. It's fucking creepy.'

I looked at Fabio while I was trying to locate a pulse and said with as much empathy as I could muster, 'Why don't you piss off over behind the counter and shut the fuck up. How does that sound?'

Fabio looked offended but could tell from the icy glare and the pissed off look he was getting from both of us that maybe discretion would be the better part of valour on this occasion and withdrew behind his counter.

I couldn't find a pulse and this bloke wasn't looking flash at all. He was pale as a ghost and his lips had started turning a light blue colour which we knew was definitely not a promising sign for any patient.

'We'd better get him on the floor and start CPR and see if we can get him cranked again,' I said to Redneck.

85

'You grab his shoulders and I'll hold his legs and then put him on the ground,' he said.

We moved to our respective positions and took hold of him as agreed.

'On three. One, two, three, GO,' I said.

With that we lifted the bloke off the chair and moved slightly forward and had him suspended about two or three feet above the floor, when his Hawaiian shirt tore from both sleeves where Redneck had his grip. The top half fell to the floor. His head actually bounced a couple of times from the impact and made a loud and sickly sounding cracking noise.

Redneck mouthed a drawn out, 'Oooooh fuck' in his guttural drawl. I lowered the legs straight away, just as Fabio called out from his vantage point behind the counter, 'Good one. If he wasn't fuckin' dead before, he will be now.'

Redneck glared at Fabio and replied, 'Don't worry about me killing this bloke. If you don't shut the fuck up, I'll come over there and kill you. You fucking germ.'

Fabio immediately shut up and looked away from him. I started CPR while Redneck got on the radio and asked D24 to call an ambulance, informing them we had an unconscious male at this location with no pulse. The operator acknowledged and a short time later came back to him with news the ambos would be there shortly.

I kept going with the heart compression and was trying to remember how many pumps of the heart you were supposed to do before giving the breaths of life. I seemed to do this stress check on my CPR procedures every time I've been called on to do it, which as far as I was concerned was far too often. I stopped after at least thirty compressions and looked at Redneck and said, 'Alright you give him mouth to mouth.'

He looked back disgusted and replied, 'Get fucked. I'm not giving the dirty prick mouth to mouth. You do it if you like him so much.'

I started laughing and turned my back on Fabio so he couldn't see and replied, 'OK you big hearted prick, I'll just keep going with the heart massage then.'

I continued for what were only a couple more groups of thirty before I said to Redneck, 'Check his pulse will you?'

He was kneeling next to the prone body of the patient and felt for a pulse on his carotid artery. He looked up surprised and said, 'He's got a pulse.'

'Fuck I'm good,' I replied.

Just as I said this, we heard an ambulance siren wailing and saw it pull up right out the front near our divvy van. Two paramedics, or ambos as they were referred to, came rushing in and took over the treatment.

'He didn't have a pulse when we got here, but I've been giving him heart massage for the last couple of minutes and I think he's got a pulse now,' I said

One of the ambos checked for the pulse while the other checked the patient's arms obviously looking for track marks. Track marks were tell-tale signs of a drug user, where they'd inject heroin or whatever else into the vein near the inside of the elbow joint. The frequent use of the needles would leave what resembled a small bruise around a miniature puncture mark.

The second ambo said, 'He's got a shitload of track marks. Must be an overdose.'

The other ambo had prepared a syringe and extracted some fluid from a small vial and injected it into the patient.

'What's that? I said.

'Narcan. It's like pure adrenalin. This stuff will have him up and running laps in a minute.'

We all waited the minute before the ambo looked at his offsider with a confused look. He gave druggie boy a second shot of Narcan. This continued until he was injected five times before he finally moaned and returned to some form of life.

'I've never given anyone five shots of Narcan to get them to come around before. He must be on some seriously bad shit,' the ambo said.

'What'll you do with him now?'

'We'll take him to the hospital and do a full check on him.'

They were preparing to load the patient onto the gurney when Fabio piped up and said, 'You might want to be careful when you lift him. He's probably already got a fractured skull.'

Redneck glared at Fabio and I looked at Redneck and started laughing which made him go red in the face and he looked like he wanted to pick up one of the washing machines and smash it over Fabio's head. Fabio sensed he was walking a tightrope and put his hands up in front of his head in mock surrender and backed away from the counter further into the shop.

We followed the ambulance to the hospital to follow up and see if we could search him for any form of identification. We got to the emergency ward and the patient was transferred from the ambo's gurney and onto a bed in a small sectioned off part of the ward. I spoke to the nurse and asked her if I could search him, just to make sure he didn't have any weapons or anything dangerous on him. The nurse agreed and said they were going to undress him anyway, as he was semi-conscious and was waiting to have a charcoal flavoured stomach pump, which I've been assured isn't a pleasant experience by numerous nurses.

Aerial view of the Walsh Street crime scene, 12 October 1988.

Crime scene photo of Walsh Street, South Yarra.

Crime scene photo of suspect vehicle on Walsh Street.

Crime scene photo of Prahran 311 van at rear of suspect vehicle.

Crime scene photo of Graeme Jensen shooting by Armed Robbery Squad
Detect Wes, 11 October 1988.

Crime scene photo of sawn off rifle in Jensen's vehicle.

Aerial crime scene photo of Bendigo Caravan Park.

Crime scene photo of Houghton's rented cabin with motorbike at the door.

Crime scene photo of weapons found in Houghton's cabin.

The plaque for my time at the Majors. The shotgun crossed with the sledge hammer and cufflinks.

Crime scene photo of 86 Chestnut Street, Richmond – home of the notorious Dennis Allen and family. Searched by many – demolished by few.

Now this was a gamechanger from manually demolishing.

Ty-Eyre Task Force team and helpers at the end of demolition. That's me in the Berwick Football shorts. Maybe the horse shoe was faulty.

Brother John Noonan working hard at demolishing 86 Chestnut Street.

Media scrum at the demolition.

It was daily coverage of the task force and demolishing a house was a first.

The Ty-Eyre Task Force – that's me in the back row, second from the right, with Sgt Geoff Calderbank on my right. John Noonan is leaning against the wall (second row far left).

That's me in the second row, third from the left. I must have not heard the instructor say, 'And don't smile or you will look like an idiot'.

The Special Duties Team were me in the middle (third row, seventh from the left), Sgt Paul Mullett (back row, second from the left), and Bill 'The Wog' Panagiotaros (second from the right, third row).

I missed the photo as I was still seconded to the Walsh Street Task Force. The boys with some of the tools of trade for the Majors; 16 pound 'key' and shotty.

Even as a child I had that 'Hey, what's going on here?'
look of a future crime fighter.

Young Joe graduates a strapping 69kg.

The 'Old Man' and I having a hit. Proof beer builds a bigger Joe.

Mum and Dad (first and second on the left) with Uncles and Aunties Des, Joy, Joe, Marg, Ida, Frank and Isabelle.

Searching for the illusive 'Rabbits' at a Pagsanjan Falls in the Philippines.

Me in the chair of future prime minister of Papua New Guinea,
Mr Bill Skate, in 1995 after leaving the police force and going out on my
own in private investigations.

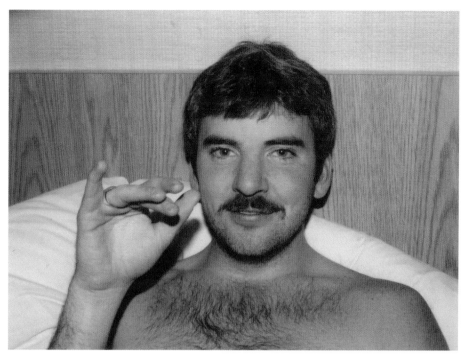

Uncle Joe could grow a moustache and has hair on his chest.
Why wouldn't I be happy!

Back at the scene of Walsh Street murders over 30 years later.

According to the nurse they didn't usually give them a stomach pump but because they didn't know what he'd taken they'd do it to be on the safe side. The nurse took off his shirt and T-shirt and pulled her head away in disgust at the overwhelming stink of body odour he exuded. One of the male orderlies came forward and started to wrestle the filthy jeans off the emaciated wreck of a body worn by the patient.

As he pulled the jeans, I noticed something sticking out the side of his jockey underwear and it wasn't his old fellow. The orderly pulled down the undies and there were about eight or 10 small plastic bags containing white powder and two bits of aluminium foil, wrapped up about an inch long.

'Aha, what have we here Watson? I said, mimicking the famous line from Sherlock Holmes.

I asked for a pair of disposable gloves and took possession of the packages from the patient. I got an envelope off one of the nurses and put the packages in it then itemised what there was. I wrote the date and time down and got the orderly to write his name down and sign the envelope to say he'd located them and given them to the police. This was to keep a chain of continuity of evidence which was important, as I had every intention of charging the patient with trafficking a drug of dependence, if they turned out to be what I thought they were, which was heroin and speed.

I asked the nurse how long before we could speak to him and she said he'd be non-compos for at least four or five hours and then he'd be discharged once his stomach had been pumped and he was up and about. I gave the nurse my card and told her I was on until 11pm and as it was only about 4.30pm could she ring me before the bloke looked like walking out. She said she would, and I took the envelope containing the suspected drugs and headed back to the office. As yet we didn't have any name or address for our duty running sheet and so referred to him as an unknown male.

True to her word, at about 9pm the nurse called the station and we got the message via D24 that the patient would be ready to go in half an hour or so. We headed straight to the hospital and spoke briefly with the nurse before being shown to the cubicle in the emergency ward where the patient was getting dressed. We walked in and introduced ourselves to the patient.

'G'day mate. Can you tell me your full name and address please?' I said.

The patient replied in a most belligerent tone, 'What for?'

'I need to speak to you in relation to a number of packets of white powder that were found in your pants this afternoon when you were brought in and before I do, I would like to know your full name and address, so I know who I am talking to.'

You're fucking joking,' he said. ' I nearly died and you pricks are going to try and charge me with something. This is fucking bullshit.'

'Listen, you're under arrest for possessing a drug of dependence. You're not obliged to say anything, but anything you do say will be taken down and given in evidence. Do you understand that?'

'This is fucking bullshit.'

He was handcuffed and escorted out of the hospital and placed in the rear of the divvy van. The nurse followed us out and asked me to give her a call when we got his details so they could update their patient records. I promised I would and thanked her for her help. We drove the patient back to the station.

On the way back Redneck said, 'Can you believe this prick? We save his life and now he's dirty because he's going to be charged with possession. Fuck me. He should be happy he's alive to be charged with anything. Ungrateful arsehole.'

I agreed wholeheartedly and we drove the short distance to the station in relative silence from then on. Once at the office the patient was seated in an interview room and I took care of the usual notifications that were required when police took someone into custody. We went out to the tearoom and made a cup of tea each and went out the back door and had a smoke. The patient was secure, as he was handcuffed to the table and the interview room had no windows, so we thought we'd let him chill out while we had a smoko.

When we finished, we walked back into the interview room and undid one set of handcuffs that had the patient tethered to the table.

Redneck said, 'Now listen here dickhead. I'll take the other handcuffs off so long as you behave. Alright?'

The patient didn't verbally respond but nodded his head in agreement and stood up and turned around so the other set of cuffs could be unlocked. Redneck undid the cuffs and put them back into their holder on his belt. I'd already done the same with the first set of handcuffs which were mine. I set up the typewriter to start the Record of Interview, which in those days consisted of three pieces of white paper with carbon paper in between each sheet. There'd be three copies of the Record of Interview, one of which would go to the patient.

I started the interview with the usual introduction detailing where we were, what day it was, who was present, the reason for the interview and the interview start time. I gave the patient another caution before proceeding. We ascertained that the patient's real name was Gary something or other and he lived in the western suburbs of Melbourne. He was definitely not impressed with being interviewed after his near-death experience and was making no attempt to cover up the contempt he had for police and more specifically us. We paused the interview and Redneck went and did a records check on Gary. In those days this consisted of a manual phone call to the Police Records Section which was referred to as IBR.

He returned a short time later with three pages of prior convictions summarised in his notebook because they didn't have computers or fax machines in stations in the early 1980s. It turned out Gary had a heap of prior convictions for drug trafficking, assault with intent to rob, burglary, theft and serious assaults spanning the last 12 years of his life, starting at age 12. He had warning flags on him for being violent and had priors for assaulting police on numerous occasions in the past. He had served time in juvenile institutions from his early teens and had done several stints in jail as well. He was currently on two sets of bail, both for drug offences.

We recommenced the interview and began questioning Gary about possessing and trafficking a drug of dependence. Gary was getting angry and refused to answer any questions and kept telling me to get fucked. I explained that we really didn't need him to say anything, as the amount of drugs found on him would be enough to get him convicted anyway, all things being equal. When he was asked what the white powder was he said, 'Eat the shit and tell me what it is you cocksuckers.'

With that he lunged out of his chair and went straight for me. Redneck moved like an obese ballerina and grabbed Gary by his long hair, as well as what was left of his Hawaiian shirt, and pulled him backwards. I was getting out of my chair and moving in to assist. Gary started throwing punches and actually connected a couple of times with Redneck's boof head. That was before he went whack and punched Gary full force in the guts, which automatically dropped Gary like a stone in a pond.

I grabbed hold of Gary's arms and handcuffed him again. He was gasping for air and we held him on the ground and told him to settle down. Redneck stayed remarkably calm, because if the shithead had have hit me in the head, I would've wanted to give it back to him.

While Gary lay on the floor getting his air back, I looked at Redneck and said, 'That was very kind of you big boy. Why didn't you punch the arsehole right in the head? What, have you gone soft?'

He looked daggers at me and then smiled and replied, 'No I haven't gone soft. And yes I would love to have knocked his fucking teeth out. However, my major concern was if I did that, I would no doubt cut my hand when I hit him and having been told by IBR that he's got Hep C, I thought it would be safer for me and hurt the arsehole more, having a big punch in the guts. Of course taking into account the fact that he has just been in hospital for the past four hours or so there's a fair chance if I hit him in the head I would've killed the dirty prick.'

I started to laugh and said, 'Why didn't you tell me the dirty bastard had Hep C?'

'You didn't ask,' he replied.

Gary was at this stage lying quietly on the floor having listened to the exchange between the two of us. When I picked him up and led him out of the interview room, he gave the death stare at Redneck and then spat a huge glob of saliva in his face. He sneered as he did it and said, 'You can get Hep C off saliva too, you fucking arsehole.'

He lunged at him and went for a jumping head butt. Redneck punched Gary in the guts with the biggest uppercut to the mid-section, which once again knocked the stuffing out of him. This time there was a little variation in his response. As he went to his knees, he vomited some gooey looking black shit all over Redneck's pants and shoes as he went down. That I believe was completely involuntary, as he was in no condition to direct his discharge. We later guessed that it was probably the remnants of the charcoal stomach flush he'd received at the hospital.

Gary was lodged in the cells after an out of sessions remand application from one of the local Justices of the Peace, or JP as they were referred to. The JP was an older professional gentleman who'd lived in that suburb all his life and had seen the influx and impact the drug trade had on his community.

When he heard the whole story he couldn't believe it. He commented on what a day the crook had had and summarised it most succinctly saying, 'So let me get this right. He dies from an overdose. Gets revived by you blokes. Goes to hospital and gets his stomach pumped. Gets arrested after that and still has the temerity to have a crack at you and then spit in your face and spew on you. Goodness me. He should be thanking his lucky stars he's alive at all.'

CHAPTER THIRTEEN

Shift from Hell

I am reasonably sure it was a weekday that had been flat out in the St Kilda area. I was working the afternoon shift divvy van and it was hot as buggery, so I am assuming it was in summer. My powers of deduction never cease to amaze. We had a bastard of a shift and before it was to finish, we'd attend two of the most distressing scenes any emergency worker can attend.

The shift started with a welfare check on a young bloke in a block of flats in Elwood just off Beach Road. Apparently, he had a history of drug use and his family hadn't heard from him for weeks. So from what we had and the location of where he lived, the signs didn't bode well for a happy ending. We got there at about 4pm and were shown to a flat. On the third floor of three of course. Remember, no one dies on the ground floor.

We trudged up the stairwell to a flat that looked very ordinary for that area. In those days not all the properties near the beach were million-dollar-plus residences. There was a great deal of rundown boarding house type accommodations, that were cheap and nasty and attracted a similar clientele.

We got to the door and were greeted by a smell that'd make a skunk baulk. There was the tell-tale sign of blow flies the size of bats hanging around the door and clinging to whoever or whatever came within range. We tried the door and it was locked. We yelled out the standard 'Police. Is anybody home?'

We banged in increasing volume with each spate of knocking on the door and yelled louder for a response. There wasn't any answer so we looked in one of the filthy little windows near the door and did a quick scan of the inside. There on a very sparsely furnished living room floor was a figure lying prostrate on the floor.

We stepped back and looked at each other as to who was going to kick in the door. We never used the shoulder to force entry because, unlike the movies, it hurt like buggery and rarely got the desired result. The size 12 was much more effective and when properly planted usually gained entry. Years later in the CIB, it was a lot more civilised. We had a 16-pound key, more commonly referred to as a sledgehammer.

So, my off-sider sinks the slipper into the door and first crack it splinters off its frame and pops the top hinge right off. It falls into the room and is left hanging by the bottom hinge. As soon as we walked in we were assaulted by a stench that seemed thick as soup. It enveloped us. It was the type of dense invisible cloud that makes breathing near impossible.

We went to where the body of what was supposed to be a male person in his early twenties was. It didn't take a medico to tell he was well and truly dead and had been that way for a few days at least. We did a quick check of the rest of the flat and found very little in the way of furniture, apart from one desk chair and what would best be described as a poor man's swag. This comprised a sleeping bag and a couple of old blankets. There was one pillow and it was stained with yellow saliva marks and probably more germs than a public toilet seat. There was no respite from the smell, and when added to the many squadrons of humungous blow flies, it was a despicable scene that revolted all the senses.

He appeared to be naked but on closer inspection that wasn't the case. He had a pair of denim shorts on that we didn't notice until we looked more closely. I'd never seen this before and can still see it in my mind. His shorts had actually been embedded in the skin and somehow the two had morphed into one. As I was checking out the body looking for any tell-tale signs of violence or suspicious circumstances, I noticed one of his eyes moved and I very nearly jumped onto my partner. He in turn jumped backwards and we both ended up falling out the door over each other back onto the balcony.

He asked me what the bloody hell I was doing and I explained as best I could that I thought one of his eyes moved. I was told in no uncertain terms there was no way his eyes were moving as he was dead as a maggot. The terminology proved unerringly accurate. We went back in and I let my partner take over the inspection of the body. I stood back half expecting some sort of alien to burst out of his guts and attack him.

He jumps back and almost cleaned me up in the process. He told me I was right and that his eyes were moving. On closer inspection there were fat white maggots moving in the eyes and the mouth. His tongue moved along with his long dead eyes under the numerous foot falls of the multitude of disgusting insects.

I nearly threw up and had to seek sanctuary on the balcony. I wasn't going to stay in that flat and do any more until we'd called the CIB. We really didn't have to call them but with a body in that bad a state of decomposition, I thought getting another opinion might help and at worst we would cover our arse in the process.

After about 20 minutes up rolls a couple of detectives from St Kilda and they looked none too pleased to have been called out in this heat and to a body. They also trudged up the stairs and we had a briefing on the balcony about halfway down the block of flats from where the body was. After a brief chat and a warning that if they had a hanky, it might be opportune to put it on as I had. Neither of them possessed a hanky and so had to go in unprotected.

As we walked in the door they both recoiled at the smell and the flies welcomed them with their grotty buzzing and hovering. They beat a hasty retreat to the balcony and couldn't believe the scene. After they'd put torn up and chewed paper into their noses, they seemed more prepared to re-enter and assess the scene. They'd asked if we knew what the cause of death was and we told them we assumed it was a drug overdose, only on the background provided by the concerned family member who called the police.

Luckily for them, they hadn't attended the flat to meet us to check on their son. We went back in and within about 30 seconds one of the detectives points his pen at a syringe that was still inserted in the dead blokes left arm. There was some dried blood in the plastic syringe, as is the case when drugs are introduced to the body intravenously. The two detectives then looked at us and shook their heads. We all retreated to the balcony again and walked away from the flat.

One of them turned to me and called me a dickhead for calling them out to an obvious overdose. He then went on to tell me it doesn't get more obvious than a syringe still hanging out of the deceased's arm. I told them I didn't even see it and after the grotesque sight of the maggots doing their thing, I really didn't look too hard at the rest.

The undertakers finally fronted, and we went through the scenario with them. They both had face masks and were at least better prepared than we were. In we went and they repelled against the smell as well. I thought that was no mean feat when you take into account some of the awful scenes they would have attended. We showed them everything and as they'd brought their stretcher up with them, they got it ready and we stayed with them in case they needed a hand. Hoping against hope they wouldn't.

They put the stretcher down next to the body and asked if we could help load him on as his stomach was bloated and he was lying on some length of old carpet. We had his feet and they took the top half and we all wore the plastic gloves the undertakers gave us, as we didn't carry anything like that in those days. They went to lift him as he seemed stuck. They had another go and as they lifted him some of the skin on his back tore and stayed with the carpet. I nearly threw up again. I withdrew and told the undertakers there was no way I was doing anything else with that body. They could call another one of their crews to help with this as I'd seen enough and was effectively withdrawing our labour from that time on.

As it turned out, they ended up getting another crew to attend and took the body out of the flat wrapped in the carpet as the only means of keeping everything together. That is without doubt the most disgusting, distressing and educational body I attended in the 10 years I was in the job. There is no training anyone can do to prepare for a scene of nature doing what nature does. For better or for worse we didn't get time to ponder this for long as we scored another job as soon as we left that one.

I couldn't believe it. We got a call via D24 for another confirmed dead body. This one was apparently an elderly female in a house in St Kilda. The next of kin was on site and there were no suspicious circumstances. So we turned up for this one and were shown the body. The poor lady was in bed and had been suffering from some form of aggressive cancer and death was expected. The family doctor attended not long after we did and was able to provide a Death Certificate for the lady.

All this meant was that there'd be no need for an autopsy or a coronial brief to be prepared, as was the case with the first body of the young bloke. So in about an hour we were clear of that address and decided it was time to get something to eat. It was about 8 or 9pm by this stage and we got takeaway from one of the many dispensaries in St Kilda. We managed to eat without either of us willing to mention anything about the first body. After we finished we hit the road and drove around Fitzroy Street checking heads and generally being happy to be out driving around in the fresh air. We couldn't believe it. To get two bodies in one shift wasn't all that outrageously out of the ordinary for St Kilda, but to have one like the first one was unique.

Without anything else of note happening for the rest of the shift, we headed back to the station and pulled the van up right out the front. We packed up our kit bag and were walking back in through the front doors when the portable radio crackled to life with a call for any unit clear in Inkerman Street St Kilda for a car accident with a possible fatality. We stopped mid-stream still in the foyer and I checked my watch. It was 10.50pm and we were due to knock off at 11pm. Should we do the right thing and head out or try and hide for 10 minutes and leave it to the night shift?

There really wasn't a choice as D24 had rung the station to pass on that there was definitely a chance of someone deceased and others trapped in their car. That was it. We flew out the front doors and chucked the kit bag back into the van and screamed off. We got to the intersection of Inkerman Street and another street which was actually the boundary between St Kilda and Caulfield's area. As we approached the scene it was like something out of a movie.

As we drove east in Inkerman Street, I saw what looked like a Volkswagen Beatle stopped at the line for the traffic lights. Partially on top of that car was another sedan with the front on the roadway. It appeared to have been flipped, landed on the Volkswagens' roof, rolled over and off, ending up on its side. The two passenger side wheels were still spinning in the air and the smell of burning rubber or brakes was strong.

A couple of other cars had pulled over and people were trying to render assistance. We came to a safe but hasty halt within about five metres of the vehicles and left our flashing blue lights on to warn any other vehicles approaching the scene. I got on the radio and told the D24 operator we were out at the job. We jumped out of our van and as we ran towards the vehicles we were approached by a bloke who told us there were people trapped in both cars and that he thought there might be two dead. I used the portable radio and asked D24 to get at least one ambulance and the Fire Brigade to attend as there may be people trapped in at least one vehicle.

We ran over and I could see there was someone stuck in the Volkswagen but he looked OK, other than the fact he couldn't get out as the driver's side door was partially collapsed around the top where the other car had landed on its roof. We kept on going and went to the car that was on its side with the driver's door on the roadway. I jumped up and stood on the passenger door which was in the air and looked inside. In the passenger seat hanging limp from the seat belt was a female in her mid-twenties. I sat in the window frame that had smashed on impact and reached down into the car and took a look at the male driver who was also limp in his seat belt.

We somehow got the young lady out of the seat belt and lifted her out of the car and with the help of one of the bystanders lowered her to the roadway, where my offsider started to do CPR.

We went back up to the car and managed to get the driver out through the passenger side window as well. I didn't want to leave him in the car, as due to the burning smell, I was worried the car might catch on fire. So as we got him out we lowered him to the roadway next to the woman and started CPR on him as well.

An off-duty nurse was on scene and she checked them both and told us they were dead. I'd got on the radio after dragging the first body out and asked them for an ambulance. I did the same when we pulled the young man out as well. Then as I was standing there thinking how bad a situation this was, another bloke yelled out that there was another car with someone trapped in it.

I hadn't seen the Torana sedan as it had recoiled backwards after impact and was a little further down Inkerman Street. It was facing west and had apparently been travelling in the opposite direction to the Volkswagen. We ran over to the Torana and the closest to me was the passenger side. I pulled open the door and could see the driver, a young female, was trapped behind the steering wheel. There was a strong smell here as well, not only of tyres and brakes, but like something was cooking.

She was conscious but was mumbling incoherently and kept saying a name over and over. I assumed she was trying to tell me her name and when I spoke to her I was telling her to hang in there as the ambulance and the fire brigade would be here soon and get her out. There was a chequered travel rug over the passenger side dashboard which I initially didn't take any notice of. The Torana was extensively damaged to the front end and had obviously hit one or both of the other cars somehow.

I went back to where the bodies of the young couple were lying and someone had covered them with blankets. Then my off sider called out and I ran back over straight away. He told me she keeps calling out a girl's name and that he didn't think it was her name.

He'd already had a look through the back seat and there seemed nothing out of the ordinary.

I leaned in and pulled on the travel rug which slipped off the dashboard. There was a shoe sticking out from under where the travel rug was. I went to pull it and to my horror it was attached to a leg. I nearly had a heart attack and jumped back which in turn frightened buggery out of my off sider.

I showed him the leg and we tried to understand what was going on. I still can't understand exactly how but the passenger had ended up under the bonnet and had part of her body on the engine which was still running.

Originally, I thought she may have gone through the glove box but after having a Torana myself, I couldn't see anything going through such a solid substance. I can't for the life of me remember what happened, but the gist of it was that somehow on impact, the bonnet had come free and the passenger had gone through the windscreen and under the bonnet, before it fell back to rest roughly in place. We hadn't noticed her leg as the travel rug covered her shoe.

When the fire brigade arrived the first thing they did was get to work with the Jaws of Life and start cutting up the Torana to get the semi-conscious driver out. She was now distraught that we'd found her girlfriend, whose name it was she had been calling out all the time. What a shocking scene. There ended up about three ambulances, a couple of fire trucks and we got some other police down to assist us.

We had to stay and wait for the driver to be cut out and taken away by ambulance. The two deceased were also taken by ambulance to the hospital. The occupant of the Volkswagen was freed and pulled up relatively well with minor injuries. The passenger in the Torana was freed from under the bonnet but was deceased. I can still recall her injuries, but it is not necessary to detail these.

We spent the next couple of hours at the scene waiting for the Accident Investigation Section (AIS) to attend and do the scene. It was during this time that we were able to ascertain how and what had happened.

The story was that the Torana was being driven by a young lady who'd been drinking and was allegedly speeding west in Inkerman Street. As she approached the red light at the intersection, the vehicle with the young married couple was travelling north on the cross street and had almost got through when they'd been T-boned by the Torana. The Volkswagen was stopped facing east in Inkerman Street at the red light and ended up with the car that'd been T-boned flipping over and landing roof first, trapping the driver. That vehicle had then slid off the Volkswagen and landed on its side.

We spent the next couple of hours until the scene was cleared of the injured, deceased and wrecked vehicles. We had to go to the morgue and go through the personal effects of the deceased before heading back to St Kilda in the early hours of the next morning. We had to track down next of kin and organise interstate police to do death notifications for the interstate couple. We either did or organised the death notice for the young female passenger in the offending Torana.

By the time all this was done, and the majority of the accident reports, statements and Inquest Brief were completed, we were done. We finally knocked off around 3 or 8 or 9pm the next day and went home. There wasn't any thought of having a beer and I know I went home and straight to bed. Unbelievably, it took me ages to get to sleep as I kept revisiting the scenes of the five dead for that shift. I felt terrible that we couldn't save the young married couple and re-experienced the feeling of utter despair at their deaths. The circumstances of the young girl in the Torana were unbelievable and I couldn't comprehend the concurrence of circumstances that cost her life in such a tragic manner.

The ambulance crews assured us the deceased would have died instantly on impact and wouldn't have known what hit them. I really hoped they'd told us the truth and weren't merely trying to assuage our obvious distress at the scene.

Once again, no training can prepare police, ambulance or fire brigade for a scene of utter destruction and death as this was. The young interstate couple had been married for about six months and were, by all reports from family and friends we spoke to, just the nicest young couple anyone would ever meet.

The young female driver of the offending car ended up with both legs badly broken in multiple places, internal bleeding among a multitude of lesser injuries. She was later charged with three counts of Culpable Driving and I'm sure she was sentenced to about eight years jail, added to the mental trauma and damage of having killed her friend and two other innocent young people. Her life was destroyed for the sake of a few too many drinks and irresponsible speed. I think of how many times I did the same thing and think 'there but for the grace of God go I'.

I watch the gruesome television adds that are on these days and always go back in my head to this scene and think if everyone got to see what I've described, they may take the privilege of driving a bit more seriously.

What a day. Five people dead in one shift and two of the scenes were two of the most gruesome I'd ever encounter.

The feelings of helplessness and despair stay with you and it's amazing what the brain stores and how vivid the recall of such incidents. I've tried to be as tactful in describing the circumstances of all five deaths but to let you know what we encountered, a certain amount of detail is required.

CHAPTER FOURTEEN

The Death of Constable Neil Clinch

Of all the stories in my police career and for that matter, my whole life, this is the hardest story I've written. I wrestled with myself whether it'd be detrimental to the family and friends of the young copper who died in this tragic set of circumstances. Then I tried to put myself in their shoes reading this and I hope they draw some comfort from it.

On 4 April 1987 I was working the district nightshift CIB car with another Senior Detective, Errol Mustafa. The nightshift CIB crews were made up of one detective from various CIB offices around Melbourne. I was stationed at Fitzroy CIB and Errol was stationed at Richmond CIB.

I'd always got on well with Errol and he was a good bloke. He had a trendy haircut like something out of Duran Duran and was what I'd classify as slightly eccentric. I didn't care as we got on like a house on fire and I could see the good bloke in him and enjoyed working and socialising with him.

This particular morning we were sitting at the office in St Kilda Road when we received a call from D24 to head to Fawkner urgently as a member had been shot during an early morning raid.

Errol was the senior member and he was also the driver that night. It was the day after my birthday and we'd tied one on to celebrate. I was still feeling decidedly ordinary and acquiesced to his wish to drive without resistance.

We flew out of the station and jumped into the unmarked sedan and Errol floored it. He drove like a rally car driver and on several occasions I wondered whether we were going to make it there in one piece. The speed limits, red lights and anything else associated with road safety were disregarded and we flew out of town with our magnetic blue light flashing on the roof.

We almost overshot the street where the raid had taken place and Errol jammed on the brakes and fish tailed the car. Thank God he was a bloody good driver and managed to correct and get back on track.

We pulled up at the address and I jumped out of the car with my heart pounding and pumped full of adrenalin. My memory of the scene isn't good, and I think there were about four or five other uniformed police in attendance. We'd got to the scene in less than 10 minutes and we beat the ambulance.

I looked at a couple of the uniform blokes and they looked to be in deep shock. I spoke to one of them and was told that a policeman had allegedly been shot by a male offender at the address. He was handcuffed and was lying on the ground. There was a rifle of some description lying nearby.

I was told the police had conducted a raid on the premises and the wounded policeman, Constable Neil Clinch, had been shot during the raid. I was told a policewoman had also fired a shot at the alleged offender when he'd levelled the rifle at her. She'd called on him to drop the weapon and he didn't comply and continued to raise it. She was said to have fired a shot as well as the offender.

I saw Constable Clinch lying on the ground near the rear right side of the house. I am pretty sure this was the south west corner and the policewoman had been standing around the corner on the south eastern side of the house. The alleged offender had come out the back door near the corner closest to Clinch.

Unfortunately, the policewoman couldn't see Clinch and vice versa. On seeing the offender raise the weapon, Clinch had tried to tackle the offender and was believed to have been shot during his attempted take down.

I picked up the rifle and checked to see if I could smell the gunpowder and then checked the chamber and realised the weapon was empty.

The policewoman was in shock and I asked one of the other coppers to take her back to the station and I'd catch up with them there.

I walked over to where Neil lay wounded on the grass. I don't remember what or how things happened, but I came to be sitting on the grass holding him. He had one eye almost closed and the other was open and I thought he was looking at me. Neil had received a shot to the head and as I sat there holding him, everything became surreal. It was like sound was muted and I was looking down from above at myself holding him.

I didn't know Neil and asked one of the other coppers what his name was. He told me and for some reason I thought it was important for him to know he was being held by someone who knew who he was.

I remember sitting there holding him like I was looking at myself through binoculars. I sat there and I really didn't know what to do. I looked around at the seemingly aimless activity of the others still there and asked someone to check on the ETA of the ambulance.

We were the detectives and we were supposed to be in charge of the scene. I remember trying not to sook up and fought a losing battle to hold back the tears. I couldn't believe it. This young bloke was a copper in uniform. We didn't get shot and look like dying.

I honestly and probably naively thought the uniform was like some mythical shield we wore and nothing would kill anyone who was brave enough to wear it. My world was being turned on its head and the harsh reality of the dangers faced by coppers in doing our job was starting to dawn on me.

I don't remember whether I was sitting down with my legs out or kneeling down and holding him. I think I took off the big overcoat I was wearing and put it under his head or over him. I really don't recall which. I was mesmerised by his eyes and the look on his face. I was saying, 'Come on mate you'll be alright. Hang on Neil. The ambulance will be here soon and they'll fix you up mate. Come on Neil, stay with me buddy.'

I looked into his eyes and I'd like to think he could hear me and know that he wasn't alone.

I didn't know him, but he wore the blue police uniform and that made him family. There was a silent but ever strong fraternity that welded coppers together in those days. It's no doubt the same in every police force, military and emergency services. Any copper reading this, no matter where he or she is, will know of the invisible bond that I'm trying to explain. I wanted him to know that he was being held by one of his brothers.

He had such a peaceful look on his face and I couldn't take my eyes off him. It was as if time had stopped. It's the sort of feeling you get when you sit absent minded staring into a log fire. There's nothing happening except the flicker of the flame over the wood but it's hypnotic. I remember watching a drop of blood run down onto to my white shirt sleeve. It was like I was watching it through binoculars in slow motion. I was mesmerised and could only keep looking at Neil and repeated my pleas for him to stay with me.

I could feel tears running down my cheeks and I had to fight an incredible internal battle not to lose it completely.

I remember looking at Errol at times during the wait for the ambulance and he gave me strength to keep composed, as best I could. He was older than me and much more experienced at holding himself together.

At this stage of my career, I was only about 24 or 25 years of age and I wasn't that much older than Neil. I was struggling with my hold on my emotions and reality. I felt like screaming out, 'What is going on here? This isn't real. We don't get shot and die.'

I was sure Neil had a faint pulse when the ambulance arrived. It'd seemed like an eternity for them to get there, but it wasn't that long. Seconds had seemed like hours and the aftermath of adrenalin and the onset of grief and shock no doubt distorted my timelines.

When the ambos arrived, they began to treat Neil and they did so like he was their little brother too. The ambulance crew understood how we were feeling and how tragic this was and did their job professionally and with all the care they could use.

I remember feeling an incredible responsibility for Neil and felt compelled to make sure he was treated properly and compassionately. They spoke to him with words of comfort, although I can't for the life of me of remember what they said.

After a short time, he was loaded onto their gurney and wheeled over to the ambulance out the front of the address. I walked with the gurney and stood by him while he was loaded into the rear of the ambulance. There must have been a television crew there at that time as I've seen the images of me walking out to the ambulance in my long overcoat next to the gurney. I can't remember whether we got a policeman to go with him in the ambulance, but I think we did.

Errol looked at me trying to hold back the tears and I remember him patting my shoulder and saying, 'Come on mate. Let's get this sorted out and get back to the station.'

The rest of what we did at the scene is a blur and I have no recollection of what transpired between the ambulance leaving and us getting back to the Broadmeadows Police Station to speak to the policewoman and establish what had happened.

We walked in and were met by the nightshift crew who were at the scene. I asked where the policewoman was and after a quick search, she was found in the female change rooms. I walked over to the door, knocked and opened it.

I remember looking at her and she was crying and obviously still in shock. I introduced myself and asked her to sit down next to me on a couple of chairs that were in the change room. I asked her to tell me what had happened at the scene and I drew a rough drawing of the house and asked her to tell me where she was and where Neil and the alleged offender were.

She talked me through what had happened and how she'd called on the suspect to drop his weapon and because he didn't and kept moving to level the weapon at her, she'd fired.

She said at the same time Neil dived on the suspect and was shot.

I asked her if she heard anyone else fire a shot and she said she didn't think anyone else had fired.

It was then that the tragedy of the situation dawned on me. I think I'd subconsciously figured it out at the scene when I saw the rifle hadn't been fired. The suspect hadn't shot Neil.

It was a tragic accidental shooting, and no one was at fault. It's what they refer to now as 'friendly fire' and although that seems like an oxymoron, I suppose it's quite accurate.

Events had conspired to put Neil in the wrong place at the exact same moment she fired. If anyone had tried to coordinate these actions again it would've proven impossible.

I know she didn't understand at the time that it was her bullet that had shot Neil. I didn't say much more, other than to tell her she'd done everything exactly as she should've. I said I wished Neil had taken the same action she did, and everything may have turned out differently.

I left her in the change room crying on the chair and made sure she had family or someone coming to look after her. My heart broke for her that morning and I hoped she knew she'd done nothing wrong and should in no way blame herself.

This was just the worst possible situation and I was working through a daze myself I think, trying to understand that this was real and not some bloody horrible dream.

The Homicide Squad detectives arrived, and I briefed them on what'd happened and the circumstances of the shooting. I don't remember much of what happened next until we left the station sometime around 10am that morning and headed back into town.

We were supposed to knock off at 7am but there was never a thought of not staying as long as we were needed. I don't know who it was, but we drove one of the Homicide blokes back into town and he made a comment about the policewoman and what he thought of them being in the job. I lost it and started shouting at him that she'd done nothing wrong and that he should shut the fuck up. We ended up dropping him off on the corner of one of the city streets somewhere and I continued to argue and vent my anger at him even after we left.

We got back to the office and signed the car and our weapons in and then Errol suggested we go for a beer. This was the police equivalent to a panacea and was invoked whenever anything particularly disturbing, dangerous or good had happened. There was no such thing as counselling in those days, or more to the point there was never any mandatory consultation after such distressing events.

We ended up driving to a pub in St Kilda somewhere and I remember we had pot after pot and hardly spoke. We sat in the pub staring out the window most of the time we were there, and it was comforting to know I had a mate there with me, without the need to engage in unnecessary small talk. We could hold the silence without it being awkward and that was good.

We must've had 10 or 15 pots of full-strength beer before we decided that was enough. The beer wasn't doing anything for me and I felt like I could've continued drinking all day and it would've have done any good or bad. When we walked out of the pub Errol reached out and shook my hand and told me to go and get some sleep.

I somehow got back to my auntie's unit in Murrumbeena where I was staying on nightshift to cut down on the travelling. I walked in there and spoke briefly to my aunty and uncle and then as I sat at their kitchen bench, I called my brother John and told him what had happened. I remember I was trying not to lose it on the phone and to keep myself composed. I failed miserably.

I couldn't compose myself for some time and had to sit there rendered mute by my emotions, listening to John trying to comfort me over the phone.

I went to bed not long after that, but I didn't sleep much as I could picture, clear as a movie, what'd happened and couldn't calm myself. I went to work that night and finished the night shift with Errol and I don't think we ever spoke about it again.

No one was able to explain or rationalise what I'd seen, and I think it was the first real challenge of my Christian faith and everything I'd been told in my younger years. I couldn't understand if there was a god, how he could let this situation happen and let it work out like it did. It didn't make sense and it still doesn't to this day.

I didn't attend Neil's funeral, which was with full police honours. I did see odd grabs on the news. I remember drinking myself to sleep that day feeling bad for not going to the funeral. But like Clint Eastwood said, 'A man's got to know his limitations'. I knew I couldn't cope going to the funeral and would only embarrass myself.

As I said previously, this is the hardest document I've ever written. I don't have to impress anyone anymore and feel no shame in my tears. They haven't been wasted and I think of them as a tribute to the dead policeman I was privileged to look after for a while.

To the Clinch family, I express my sincere condolences and hope there's some comfort in knowing what happened that morning.

To me, it looked like he was having a peak at heaven when I was with him and it must've looked alright, because he had the most peaceful look on his face and in his eyes. That's what's been the saving grace for me to this day. I hope I see whatever he was looking at when I go.

CHAPTER FIFTEEN

The Major Crime Squad

The day I started at the Major Crime Squad was a day I'd been looking forward to since I'd won the vacancy for the Senior Detectives spot.

I remembered walking in to the 11th Floor and was warmly greeted by Col Florence and introduced to all the crew. There were about seven crews comprised of a detective sergeant and two senior detectives.

Tony Thatcher, commonly referred to as Thatch, was another senior detective who started that day as well. I didn't know him at that stage, but I certainly got to know him over the next couple of years and he was another top bloke. He was a funny bastard and was somewhat non-descript for a Major Crime Squad Detective. He was about my height, slim and had slightly protruding top teeth, which made it look like he was always smiling. Even when things were going poorly, Thatch always looked happy, which at times struck me as strange or inappropriate, but that was him.

That first day I met my Detective Sergeant, Peter Spence or Spencey. He was huge. He was about 6'4" and was built like a UFC fighter. He had the craziest eyes I'd seen and when I saw him mad they looked like golf balls and instantly frightened shit out of the poor hapless crook or copper who was the subject of his bad mood.

He spoke in a fashion that made people listen. Apart from the fact he was huge and looked slightly crazy, people made the effort and would listen strenuously to hear what he said.

I was shown around and Spencey decided we should go for a drive. Me being the new bloke, I drove and Spencey folded himself into the passenger seat. As we drove along something happened to attract his attention and he instructed me to pull over a car in the old City Road area near where the Casino is now. I flashed the headlights and tooted the horn while Spencey held his Freddie out the window.

This worked and the suspect car pulled over to the side of the road and we pulled up behind it in our unmarked Ford sedan.

Spencey stepped out of the car first and I had my door on the road side and so had a look to make sure traffic was clear before I opened it. I waited for a car to pass and then made my move and opened my door. Next thing, BANG.

I shit bricks and fell back into the car as my door was smashed into and left hanging by one hinge. Thank God I didn't have a good grip of the door handle, or he probably would've ripped my arm off with the door.

As I was trying to put all the pieces together as to what had just happened, I looked over to the passenger side and saw Spencey lean down and put his head in the doorway on his side and with his deliberate, deep voice said, 'What the bloody hell was that?'

I thought I was in deep shit and that my Major Crime Squad tenure may have just become the shortest in the squad's history.

I thought an attempt at humour may be the right tack to loosen up a very bad situation for me. I looked at Spencey and said, 'That prick just stole my door' and gave a half-hearted laugh.

He looked at me without speaking for what seemed like a year and then simply unfolded out of the doorway again and went to speak to the offending driver.

It turned out I'd let the car pass but hadn't noticed he was towing a trailer and so when I opened my door the trailer had taken it out.

You don't have to be dead to be stiff and the driver of the car that stole my door was probably as stiff as you could get.

It turned out he was unlicensed and had no registration for the car or the trailer. I couldn't believe it and felt bad for the poor bastard.

We had to stay there for ages and wait for a uniform sergeant to attend to do the police accident report.

So big Spencey wasn't at his humorous best for a couple of hours, until we got back to the Majors office.

It didn't take long for word to get around that the new bloke had bingled one of the cars on his first day. I also had shit hung on me because I had to charge the driver with traffic offences relating to his lack of licence and registration.

So not only had I caused one of the squad's cars to be towed away, my first brief at the Major Crime Squad was a traffic brief. It was tantamount to working in a tutu to do a traffic brief in the CIB, let alone the Majors.

Col Florence laughed his head off and led the unmerciful shit hanging that I had to endure that day. Luckily I knew a lot of the blokes and took the roasting in good humour.

So after spending the first day doing traffic reports, at about 4pm out came the cans, as they had cause to do nearly every day I was there. The Majors was a most sociable squad and luckily I was a most sociable bloke.

So that was the first day at the Major Crime Squad and it set the scene for some hard work, long hours and some fantastic nights on the turps.

Somehow, we made it through our troublesome initiation to the Majors and I still laugh when I think of it. Not long after we got there, we were placed in the full time care of Detective Sergeant Peter Spence. So, Thatch and I were put through our paces and maintained the sociable responsibilities of the squad.

I remember after I'd been there for about a month, I went down to the Homicide Squad to see my brother. When I walked in he looked at me and asked what the hell had happened to me. I asked what he meant, and he pointed towards my somewhat inflated girth and the ruddiness of my complexion.

I'd been on the turps solid since I got there and had spent more than one night sleeping at the office and even under my desk on the odd occasion. I even had my clothes sent out for dry cleaning, including jocks and socks, as I wasn't getting home to do the washing myself.

So, after that I decided to do something about it. No I didn't consider getting off the grog or anything quite so drastic.

I got back into the weights and the running, in between the working and drinking.

Slowly but surely, I got back my chiselled physique and lost my guts, not without some extremely hard workouts with Peter Spence. He worked out like he drank. Hard and fast and set a cracking pace with little or no break between reps and some brutal circuit work, which I must admit did do wonders for me.

CHAPTER SIXTEEN

Australia's Most Wanted Versus the Armed Robbery Squad

The shooting of Graeme Jensen in Narre Warren at approximately 3.30pm on 11 October 1988 by members of the Armed Robbery Squad was said to be the precursor to the Walsh Street murders of Constables Steve Tynan and Damien Eyre. If we had a crystal ball in those days then what I am going to describe now may have changed and even prevented Walsh Street.

The circumstances months earlier surrounding the arrest of Russell 'Mad Dog' Cox and Raymond John Denning, if lady luck had intervened, may have changed history and the body count from those turbulent years, pre and post Walsh Street.

These two were arrested on Friday 22 July 1988 at the Doncaster Shopping Centre after a brief and one-sided shoot out with the Armed Robbery Squad.

Cox and Denning were seasoned and dangerous crooks who were both on the run and they occupied the top spots on the country's Most Wanted lists.

Cox in particular was a murderer and carried out many daring armed robberies, showing his penchant for violence and disregard for the lives of anyone in his way. He had a chequered history and one of his worst priors would have been allegedly having an affair with a notorious lady of crime. Anyone who could 'date', for want of a better word, the cycloptic Medusa of the crime world, had to be a desperate and careless individual.

Cox had served time with Denning at Katingal jail in Queensland in the mid-1970s. He escaped from Long Bay jail in 1977 and was free and on the run from police all over Australia for the next 11 years, ending with his apprehension at Doncaster Shopping Town in the company of Denning. He was the prime suspect in the 1983 shooting murder of Ian Revell Carroll at Mt Martha in Victoria.

He was ably assisted by his 'barrel girl' Helen Deane, who was a trained nurse and no doubt that skill would have come in handy for Cox and his various associates over his years on the run.

She was the sister-in-law of Ray Chuck Bennett, who was the brains behind the Great Bookie Robbery in Melbourne in 1976.

It's funny how things work out, but I went to Manila in the Philippines in 1982, the year after I had graduated from the police academy. Little did I know that Dennis Smith owned and ran one of the bars we went to in Manila that year. It was the first time I had been overseas and so when we learned of the Aussie Bar we thought we had better go and check it out, obviously out of some inadvertent sense of Aussie patriotism.

It is amazing that the further you go from home, the more the attraction there is in seeking out and being in the company of other Aussies. Smith allegedly cleaned or laundered some of the proceeds from the Bookie Robbery through his purchase of the Aussie Bar.

We had heard an advertisement in Melbourne for what we thought was to go and shoot rabbits at Pagsanjan Falls. So I said to a mate of mine, 'that sounds alright'. We book and take off for our shooting trip to Manilla. It turns out the rabbits at these falls were actually rapids and I felt like the biggest dickhead of all time when we got there and asked where we hired the rifles and were handed paddles instead by some bemused Pilipino.

To add insult to idiocy, while checking out a number of the 'girly bars' in Manilla, I couldn't believe how cluey some of these sheilas were. At nearly every one I was greeted with 'Hey GI Joe. You want girl. I love you long time'.

I remembered looking at my mate and asking him if he had told them my name. How the bloody hell did they know I was Joe? Of course, it turned out that the yanks had been stationed in the Philippines during WWII and were referred to by the locals as GI Joes. We ended up going on tours of Corregidor and Bataan Islands while we were there. So the chance of me recognising Mad Dog Cox or any other bad bastard from Australia at that stage was minimal.

As I was saying, coming in at the number two spot on the Country's Top 10 Most Wanted was Raymond John Denning.

Denning was born in Port Kembla in the southern outskirts of Sydney in 1951. From 1966 to 1972 he was charged with offences ranging from car theft, burglary and serious assault and did pretty well only receiving probation, bonds and finally short stints in jail. He did short time in Adelaide and Queensland.

In 1973 he had served his apprenticeship and graduated to being a serious crook. He was convicted in Sydney for Armed Robbery and associated offences and was sentenced to 13 years with a non-parole period of five -and-a-half years.

Whilst serving that sentence in the Parramatta Prison he seriously assaulted a prison warden during an escape attempt. It was a serious hiding and the poor bloke never worked again and died as a result of his injuries four years later. Denning was sentenced to life imprisonment in 1976. He was transferred after that assault to Maitland Jail, where he escaped in 1977. Denning was sentenced in 1978 to another six years on top of his original life sentence. I don't know how that would've worked. What do they do, hold the body for six years after you die? Anyway, I am sure the intent was to send a message that he'd be punished for his conduct, no matter what the original term was.

In reality, no one ever served life and could be out in 14 years or so with good behaviour and less if you found God. God obviously spent most of his time in prisons because heaps of crooks found him there when I was buggered if I could find him on the outside.

Denning didn't seem to want to do that much jail time and in 1980 was the first person to escape from Grafton Jail in the 80 years it'd been in existence.

He was regularly taunting police whilst on the run and committed at least two armed robberies in Queensland and did very well out of them. He stayed on the run until November 1981 when he was arrested in Sydney and was back in jail.

The authorities managed to keep him locked up until 14 July 1988 when he once again took unauthorised leave from the minimum-security prison at Goulburn Correctional Centre.

It took Denning eight days to get in contact with Cox, as they'd formed some form of robber's club years before and had set up a secret method to get in touch with each other after a job or an escape. Both of which were plentiful.

It's quite amazing that Cox had been on the run for the past 11 years and Denning did what no police force in Australia could do. Find and meet with Cox.

They agreed to meet at Doncaster Shopping Town, a well to do suburb of Melbourne, after a phone call and both went there in separate vehicles.

As it turned out, a Brambles Armoured van crew noticed the two, apparently sitting off their truck. They notified the Armed

Robbery Squad, who left their offices at St Kilda Road and flew out to Doncaster loaded up with Remington 12-gauge pump action shotguns, ballistic vests, and their standard issue Smith & Wesson 38 calibre revolvers.

I'm not sure how many attended, but I would imagine the whole squad rolled out to such a call and had the area well and truly covered before their intercept. Or did they?

When they got there, they were in turn noticed by Cox and Denning.

Denning was the first to break cover and attempted to drive away from the police cars. One of the Armed Robbery Squad vehicles rammed his car head on and the 'Robbers' as they were referred to in the job had weapons trained on him before he could do anything and was quickly arrested.

Cox saw what happened with Denning and made his move. He sped off and drove like a mad man, no pun intended, around the car park and away from pursuing detectives. He executed a U turn and drove straight at the Armed Robbery Squad Detectives. A shotgun blast took out one of the tyres as he persisted to try and escape with a pistol in one hand and the steering wheel in the other. Another shotgun blast took out the windscreen. Cox lost control and crashed into a wall in the car park after bouncing off another parked car and was overpowered and arrested. He didn't get the time or the opportunity to use his shooter and who knows what would've happened if he did. Denning and Cox were then transported back to the offices of the Armed Robbery Squad at St Kilda Road.

Being a glass half full sort of bloke, I reckon these two should count themselves as a couple of the luckiest blokes in history. I think more shots were fired that day than in the taking of Bagdad and they managed to miss all of them.

I remember that afternoon well. I was sitting at my desk at the Major Crime Squad preparing for the obligatory beer at either our office or the Armed Robbery Squad across the hall from us.

There was notification that most of their blokes would be tied up, as they had caught two armed robbers staking out an armoured van at a shopping centre. They didn't know who they were at the time of their arrest and apparently took some convincing that one of the blokes they had was in fact Russell Cox.

One of the detectives later told me that they had Cox in an interview room and were vigorously questioning him when he made comment that it was their lucky day or words to that effect. He then told them he was Russell Cox. Yeah right.

At some point someone thought they better check the story out and took a set of fingerprints and had them walked through the police criminal records section at St Kilda Road.

When the identity of Cox was confirmed the whole atmosphere changed in the Armed Robbery Squad. There were scenes of jubilation and one of their blokes came running into our office to tell us they had caught Mad Dog Cox.

We were even invited to come over and have a look at him in the interview room. When we got there, we were presented with a scene I will never forget. Cox was posing for photos with the Armed Robbery Squad Detectives, in similar fashion to a successful football team photo. Cox looked a little bit worse for wear and had obviously incurred some injuries during his violent and adrenalin pumped arrest.

In one photo Cox was posing holding one of the squad shotguns. What a sport he turned out to be. Wouldn't you think that Australia's Most Wanted would be too busy to have pictures taken by the coppers who arrested him? Not Russell. He was just one of the boys.

Unfortunately for him he was one of the boys on the wrong side of the event management team that day. I am pretty sure he may have even joined our boys for a beer during the not for the public shots.

At the time I was stoked for the Robbers as well. What a great pinch.

I didn't know the whole story at that stage and thought they must've known who they had when they arrested them. I don't know what made Cox reveal his true identity, but I reckon a few shotgun blasts in his direction during the arrest may have helped. He may also have assumed that Denning had 'ratted' him out and organised the meeting as a means to getting him for the police.

During the processing and subsequent identity checking, another detective from the Robbers popped over for a quick beer and told us that they had identified Cox's off sider as Raymond John Denning.

My ears pricked up when his name was mentioned, as I was the holder of the Arrest and Extradition Warrant for Denning. Detective Sergeant Peter Spence and I went over to the Robbers' office and enquired as to what had been done with Denning. We asked whether they had searched his vehicle and were told they had.

After such an eventful and successful day, it was time to relax and have a beer or three hundred and celebrate their win. There would have been Armed Robbery Squad detectives all over the country having a celebratory drink and cursing the fact the bloody Mexicans (as us Victorians were referred to by interstate forces) had got him instead of them.

Some two weeks later, Peter Spence got to look at a bag of what was found in Cox's vehicle. It was in a plastic bag handed to him by a special task force that had been working on Cox for ages.

There were the usual bits of paper and crap from the glove box. I saw a lawn mowing service receipt and called the phone number for the lawn mowing service and ascertained he'd cut the grass at an address in the last couple of days prior to the shootout and was paid in cash. I got the address from him and whatever details he had of whoever he had spoken to or seen at the address when he went there.

He described Russell Cox but referred to him by another name. Peter Spence organised a Search Warrant and we took out a number of crews and surrounded the house. We had already made enquiries as to the owner of the house, the usual pre raid checks, and I can't for the life of me remember what we were told, but we raced out to the address and were seriously tooled up with our shotguns, revolvers and sledge hammers.

Even though we were flat out, he still had time to swear the warrant as was required. Little did we know that police in the world of the future would either lose that skill or just could not be bothered doing it. It was basic detective work. Anyway, that is still in the future at this stage.

We crashed in the door and were screaming 'Police' and whatever else we yelled, to no-one as it turned out. We searched the unit and it had been cleaned out. Everything was gone. It looked like it had been packed up in a hurry and whoever was there didn't stick around. I searched one of the built-in wardrobes and we found a false back compartment which was ajar. Whoever had left made sure he took the contents of this false cupboard with him. At the bottom of the cupboard was a magazine from a M16 or similar looking military rifle. When we found the magazine, the import of what we had found started to hit home.

Whoever had lived there had either ran with or been associated with the two most wanted crooks in the country. The assumption is obviously that like attracts like, and the person that had fled was also a violent and desperate man.

We had missed him as he'd bailed out of that place, apparently in a hurry on the day of Cox's arrest at Doncaster. No doubt he would've heard it on the news and thought discretion may be the better part of valour and hightailed it, rather than wait for the 16 pound key preceding a horde of Armed Robbery Squad detectives tooled up and ready for bear.

He need not have worried to get out in the hurry he did with all his belongings stuffed into garbage bags.

It turned out to be a crook by the name of Santo Mercuri, funny enough, who was a violent, desperate and dangerous armed robber. It sounds so cliché to describe people like that but it doesn't do them justice. They were people who thrived on terrorising innocent people doing their banking and gave no thought to the trauma they would cause for the poor victims of their stick ups for the rest of their lives.

The intelligence gleaned later found that Mercury had allegedly committed armed robberies with members of the Flemington Crew, most notably Frank Valastro, Mark Moran and Russell Mad Dog Cox.

During one stick up they committed in 1987, they fired around 60 shots from an M16 or similar type military rifle, as well as shotgun shells.

Valastro came to grief at the hands of the SOG during a raid on his house not long after that and so his career came to a sudden end.

I have wondered many times what may have happened, or more importantly not happened, if the enquiries we made two weeks after the arrest of Cox and Denning had been done on the day of their arrest.

Maybe they would have got Santo Mercuri then and found what he had in his possession. If that had have happened, the bullet wound to Mercuri's hand, that was incurred when he was shot by Dominic Hefti during the Brunswick armed hold up, would have been discovered. Dominic Hefti was a security guard shot dead during that exchange of gunfire.

Maybe they or we might have found some evidence from that job and changed the thinking on who had committed it.

Maybe Jensen would not have been targeted for that job and maybe he would not have been shot then.

Maybe Walsh Street would not have happened and maybe two policemen might be alive today.

Maybe Jedd Houghton and Gary Abdullah may be alive. Maybe is a big word, even though it does not sound all that important.

No one has the ability to go back in time and things invariably conspire at the time of their occurrence to impede the perfect outcome. No one could have known what the relevance and importance of finding Santo Mercuri was at that stage.

As it was, it was another five years before he was subsequently captured and convicted of the murder of Dominic Hefti and two counts of Armed Robbery surrounding the circumstances of his shooting and his getaway.

It turned out that Raymond John Denning became an informer for a copper from New South Wales after his arrest and incarceration as a result of that day.

He reckons he changed his attitude to Cox after they were in jail in Melbourne together. He recounted how Cox had laughed when he heard Graeme Jensen had been shot after being the chief suspect for the murder of Hefti. He laughed and told Denning they had got the wrong man. That was the first time Denning knew Cox and Mercuri, and not Jensen, had done that stick up.

CHAPTER SEVENTEEN

Graeme Jensen Versus the Armed Robbery Squad

Now the relevance between the fatal shooting of Armaguard security guard Dominic Hefti becomes apparent. The Armed Robbery Squad had been investigating a number of serious armed robberies, one of which involved the Hefti shooting during an armed raid on a Coles Supermarket cash delivery in Brunswick in July 1988.

The operation into this and a series of other violent armed robberies was Operation No Name and was centred on a growing number of jobs being attributed to a gang referred to by the Armed Robbery Squad as The Flemington Crew.

Graeme Jensen and Victor Peirce were strongly suspected of being involved and Jensen was placed under covert surveillance.

The rest of the Flemington Crew were to come to prominence, not only for a majority of the crimes attributed to them but, more importantly for me, the deaths of Constable Tynan and Eyre.

Jensen was moving around a lot as he was an active criminal and was switched on at all times and didn't want to be easily found should anyone, especially the police, try and locate him, for whatever reason.

At approximately 3.30pm on the afternoon of 11 October 1988, Jensen had left an address in Narre Warren and driven his girlfriend's car to a mower shop in Webb Street near the Princes Highway intersection.

There were apparently five covert police following Jensen unbeknownst to him. He walked into a mower shop and was followed by at least one undercover policeman. This was done to confirm his identity for the Armed Robbery Squad detectives who were hiding in their unmarked cars nearby.

Jensen walked back to his car, got in and was intercepted by members of the Robbers, who subsequently shot and killed him. He was hit by a slug from an SG shotgun shell, fired by one of the detectives as he allegedly tried to escape.

The story was that he was armed with a 22 calibre sawn off rifle found on the driver's side floor of the car he was driving. There were allegations that the rifle was planted on Jensen by a member of the Robbers after his death, when a towel was taken out of one of the unmarked police cars and placed over his body. The rifle was alleged to have been in that towel and planted to justify the shooting.

I have recently read an account of what was alleged to have happened that day by a former policeman who was part of that surveillance crew.

Malcolm Rosenes ended up being jailed for drug offences many years after the Jensen shooting in 1988. His story has been penned by a disgraced former solicitor and convicted drug trafficker, Andrew Fraser, in his book *Snouts in the Trough*.

In that book, it's alleged that Rosenes and his crew were never warned by the Robbers that they intended intercepting Jensen that day and the manner in which they attempted the mobile intercept was against police procedures and dangerous to the welfare of the surveillance crews. This was because without knowing what was going to happen, they were not able to ensure they were out of the line of fire when the shooting started.

He further alleges he saw one of the Robbers plant the rifle in Jensen's car after the shooting.

I can't confirm or negate Rosenes' account of what he says happened that day, as I wasn't there and don't know Rosenes. I did meet Andrew Fraser when he was representing some of his clients that I had charged at odd intervals during my career in the police force. His conviction and imprisonment for attempting to import a commercial quantity of drugs was not surprising. Somehow the two of them met after their respective terms of incarceration and Fraser was asked to write Rosenes' account of his time in the police force.

Rosenes also makes more serious allegations that the running sheets or surveillance logs of that day, along with the statements of all the surveillance police present, were taken from his locker once the legitimacy of the Jensen shooting was being investigated.

He alleges his statement for the inquest and later trial was taken by members of the Robbers at the office of the Armed Robbery Squad.

He alleges their statements were concocted to mirror the evidence of the detectives who were subsequently charged with Jensen's murder.

In effect, they were allegedly coerced into signing statements that all stated they saw nothing of what took place that day.

Whether that is true or not, I don't know.

The eight detectives who were charged either had their charges dropped by the Director of Public Prosecutions (DPP) and one was presented for trial and acquitted by a jury.

I remember the Police Association used enormous resources in time and money in ensuring their successful defence against the charges. There was a public outcry that alleged that not all of the evidence was tendered during the trial and apparently the offices of the DPP were broken into before or during the trial.

Apparently, evidence relating to the prosecution case against the members of the Armed Robbery Squad was stolen and never recovered.

No one was charged with the break in and theft of the evidence.

It was widely speculated that the shooting was not legit and that the Robbers had murdered Jensen in cold blood. They had allegedly planted a 'throw away' firearm into his car after the shooting.

A 'throw away' was common vernacular for a weapon dubiously obtained by police and held by them until it was 'needed'. Such as in circumstances surrounding the allegations of the Jensen shooting.

The Armed Robbery Squad was notorious among criminals and the Civil Liberties advocates for their modus operandi. Numerous allegations leading up to the Jensen shooting were being made about the circumstances of other shootings.

The shooting deaths of Mark Militano and Frank Valastro at the hands of the squad were also the topic of hot conversation in and out of the police force.

The result of the latter of these shootings being Valastro allegedly resulted in some of his associates making a pact to take out two police for any one crook shot by the police.

Some suggested that because the Robbers had been unimpeded in their course of conduct pertinent to those two shootings, then Jensen's shooting would pose no problem either.

A solicitor at court one day asked someone whether the Armed Robbery Squad were told their title was a noun and not a verb.

It is interesting that the Armed Robbery Squad was disbanded years later, after a number of detectives were charged with assaulting an offender. There were covert cameras installed in the

interview rooms and it was all over the news media about the
job the Office of Police Integrity did. At least when the Armed
Robbery Squad was at their best we all lived in a safer place.
Crooks were turned off committing armed robberies and I think
all violent crimes took a dive in the statistics.

Now all we all have to answer to ourselves as we think about this
is what price are we willing to pay to win back the streets? Are we
as prepared now to give unconditional endorsement to the police
to 'go hard' and forget the consequences?

Whatever the truth about the Graeme Jensen shooting, the
facts as they stand are that it was a legitimate shooting of a suspect
armed with a firearm by police in the execution of their duty.
That's that. The impact it had on the police force and the lives of
police and the community as a whole is also pretty sure.

The shooting of Graeme Jensen led to the shooting murder of
two young constables, who had done nothing to warrant such
action and retaliation. The Armed Robbery Squad was and will
always be at the forefront of the story and the aftermath. You make
up your own mind whether it was for better or for worse. I am no
apologist for police and that's why I have provided two polarised
accounts of the suspicion and innuendo surrounding the Armed
Robbery Squad and the Jensen shooting.

CHAPTER EIGHTEEN

The Politics of Task Force

My brother John Noonan was a Detective Senior Sergeant at the Homicide Squad. He and his crew had attended the scene of the Jensen shooting and was the 'on call' crew which responded to the Walsh Street shootings.

John was subsequently promoted to Detective Inspector not long into the task force and so he and another inspector were of equal rank, although the other bloke had seniority on his side. I will refer to this other bloke as Inspector X, in case he is feeling delicate these days. The two of them seemed to get on well at the start of the job, but within weeks the wheels started to loosen on their wagon.

John was the dominant personality on the task force and made no bones about it. The other was quieter and was more of a leadership by consultation sort of guy. John had more of a didactic management paradigm in that he was the decision maker and that was that. I learnt 'didactic management paradigm' when I did Uni a few years back and I have tried to use it anywhere I could.

Of course, John sought and was given the opinion of those that had specialist information and wasn't completely totalitarian in his leadership. He had an incredible ability to let the job completely engulf him and everything else came a long second. His approach and total commitment were hard to keep up with, so there were those that liked it and those that loathed it. I was mostly non-committal as he was my big brother so what could I say. I was more into doing my own thing, working hard and playing hard. Leadership in those days was not on my radar. I was busy looking after myself. That was hard enough.

As the police force was ruled by a hierarchical structure, it was easier for him to dominate those around him. He was and still is a big bloke standing about six feet tall and is very well built. He had a lightning fast temper and was at times intolerant of what he perceived to be stupidity or incompetence.

He favoured a hard response to the slayings and it wasn't a hard task to find allies. Everyone in the police force and most of the community of Victoria, and in fact the country, were appalled by the murders and wanted justice. I remember the flood of well wishes and messages of solidarity from interstate and international police departments. I think it speaks volumes for the importance that was placed on the Task Force. From our point of view, they waited an inordinate amount of time to form it; they failed to provide adequate resources to enable it to carry out the most basic of functions; they stepped back and effectively abdicated any responsibility for overseeing the day-to-day operations, interactions and conflict, and they placed unrealistic objectives and unrealistic timeframes in which to achieve them. They wanted this job wrapped up post haste but did nothing to facilitate the success of the task force from its infancy. I think nothing that starts off poorly will ever deliver anything of value.

In light of these limitations, the fortitude, commitment, self-depravation and professionalism displayed by most of the task force members, most of the time, was truly remarkable and shouldn't be underestimated.

135

It is vitally important to take the personalities out of the equation, where possible, when critiquing the task force and its achievements and failures. It took a chunk of many people's lives that we could never get back.

Time spent away from wives, husbands, mothers, fathers, children and family in general are priceless sacrifices. The total and heart-felt commitment to the cause we were investigating was awe inspiring. I don't think I could do it again if I'd been called on now.

Although hopefully the police department has got smarter and learned from Walsh Street and the aftermath. Hopefully.

I don't think it's possible to be so close to tragedy, without absorbing some of it in the very tissue that makes us what we are. It is tantamount to cleaning a chimney and expecting not to get any soot on you in the process.

Grief, sorrow and heartbreak aren't inanimate emotions. They have their own feel and can be passed on with close contact.

I think there's a cumulative process to policing in that with every death, whether violent and premeditated, to accidental or unintentional; every act of inane violence, every act of incomprehensible depravity, or any instance evoking supreme emotion and grief; a little bit is absorbed with contact.

The management and leadership of the Task Force was plonked on the backs of these two blokes. The expectations of a police force, a state and a country rested with them.

This was to be the largest police investigation ever conducted and it had to be successful. The hierarchy didn't care how and I believe they didn't comprehend the enormity of the task they bestowed on these two blokes.

The response had to be strong but fair: it had to be rapid, but well planned; it had to be successful no matter what.

In my opinion there wasn't enough leadership shown to keep the task force moving forward. The split between the leadership effectively split the task force in two. In my opinion, there were a number of senior police that should have intervened and sorted the strife out early in the piece before it got to the point it did.

I reckon a lot of the blame falls on the leadership group at the time. They should have had their finger more on the pulse and made sure the split never happened and the resultant animosity between the two groups never got to where it did.

If they were too busy or otherwise engaged, which I would find hard to believe, then they should have ensured others within that same group were suitably involved.

I imagine anyone on the leadership group didn't get to work each day and have the To Do List on a note pad in front of him. There could have been important stuff like:

1. Pick up dry cleaning.
2. Get car washed.
3. Tell the media we don't have enough of everything.
4. Plan holiday.
5. Don't forget to sort out the leadership bullshit at the new task force. Ty Eyre?

The office we were given was inadequate and we had to go through the interruption and hassle of moving the whole thing after a matter of weeks.

The trouble was in keeping them moving forward at a measured and considered pace. The temptation was for individuals to fly off on their own and make enquiries or comments that were not approved by the Task Force.

This was evidenced by continuous intelligence that the Task Force was telling people that we wanted to kill them, rather than speak to them. No doubt a novel approach, but not right.

I have no doubt, especially at the start, when emotions were sky high and the want for revenge was at its peak, that some in or close to the Task Force were making those comments. They let their heart rule their head and all it served to do was instil a level of distrust and fear into the very people we needed to talk to.

Unfortunately, the bravado and primitive instincts of some took over and they wanted to be the tough guys running around telling people they were going to kill them.

Whenever we were feeling knackered, which was regularly after working monstrous hours with little or no days off, we would be shown the scene photos to remind us and relight the fire under us.

That was the intention anyway. Whether it worked after the first couple of times I am not sure.

I know that I ended up not wanting to see the scene photos any more than I had to, as they were obviously distressing.

We encouraged each other by camaraderie, banter and enjoying a dark sense of humour that most coppers have.

The team had to manipulate and improvise what was out-dated and incompatible software and hardware and get it to do what they wanted it to.

For instance, when all the Intelligence Reports were entered into the system, they were able to utilise a data interrogation program that could search by key words. This may seem pretty basic information technology today, but in 1988 it was cutting edge and they did a remarkable job.

The days and nights became one for the first three of four months and we worked long and exhausting hours.

I think we averaged in the vicinity of 18 hours a day during that time. The office became more home than home and we worked, slept, ate and lived the job. I was a big drinker prior to the Task Force and relied on alcohol more than I should have. It helped me be the funny man, but more importantly from my point of view, it helped me sleep.

Let's look at the resourcing of the task force and you may start to comprehend the difficulties that were encountered from the start.

An army marches on its stomach and if the supply lines aren't up to scratch, the army stops. While the department allocated plenty of physical resources, the behind the lines support were not there to maximise any intelligence that was gathered.

From 12– 18 October no word processing operators were allocated to the investigation. Now computers were still relatively new technology and none of the investigators had a clue how to use them. John Noonan submitted a formal request on 15 October for Word Processing Operators (WPOs) which resulted in six well-intentioned but untrained temporary staff being provided. They found it hard trying to keep up with the copious amount of intelligence reports that were flooding into the Homicide Squad during the days prior to the Task Force being established.

To give you some appreciation of the amount of intelligence reports received, there were 350 between 12–13 October. From then on it averaged 150 intelligence reports a day.

This is where it was critical to have a system that could cope with the volume and then enable the search functionality required. For instance, we could then search 'Red car in Carlton' and all the red cars mentioned in Intelligence Reports (IRs) would pop up on the screen with their reference numbers for retrieval. The whole report would also be able to be read straight from the database. That was the theory.

The Information Technology Division (ITD) was largely unable to assist due to them not having the required skills and competencies. The world of technology was not what it is today and we either had the monetary or specialist resources that would be allocated if this happened today. I am sure these people were also well intentioned but just under resourced. Pirate software was obtained to enable data entry and basic interrogation functions.

On 27 October ITD provided a Local Area Network (LAN) system after a request from the Task Force, as what we had was useless. The LAN system provided two personal computers for input and two for searching. There were two entire days lost during the setting up of the LAN.

On 21 November, due to the untested Text Retrieval Package that had been provided, the system crashed. There was bedlam.

The Task Force computer system was down until 28 November and we were having to read IRs as they came in and try and allocate them manually.

The delay was partly due to installing the new programme and partly due to the time consuming and tedious process of applying for the authority to approve the additional cost.

Our analysts had requested a backup be installed from the start of the installation. It was not done and on 29 December the system blacked out again and we lost over 300 statements that had been entered.

After a month or so, the Task Force was moved to more spacious offices situated on the 14th floor at St Kilda Road. It was a million-dollar view that we never appreciated at the time.

Drinking had been replaced with mental fatigue that helped me sleep. We hardly imbibed at all and when we did have the odd beer, that was all it took and we were two pot screamers and wanted to go to bed.

The social life I enjoyed at the Major Crime Squad came to a sudden halt. As the hours morphed into days and they in turn into weeks, the grind was starting to have its effect on people. Tempers became frayed and everyday things people did or said started to grate on other's nerves.

The paths of our leaders were starting to diverge and the further decaying of that relationship would bring with it serious and inappropriate consequences. As the weeks became months, some people's ability to maintain the intensity and the hours began to wane.

I've read numerous books on the Walsh Street murders and found some to be most confusing. I think too much detail can be included which if you were not living the investigation every day and didn't know all the players; it's hard to keep up with. I will give a summary of the important times during the investigation such as arrest dates, interview dates, moments or occurrences of import and dates of shootings involving police and suspects.

CHAPTER NINETEEN

Let Me Tell the Story of a Man Named Jedd

Jedd Houghton was alleged to have been one of the triggermen at the murders of Steve Tynan and Damien Eyre.

He was a convicted car thief and apart from that had no prior convictions for anything that would suggest he would take part in such a vicious attack on two young coppers.

Straight after the murders, his name had been mentioned in tip offs to the police as being involved at Walsh Street.

The Armed Robbery Squad quickly produced numerous surveillance shots of three men involved in casing a Boronia bank along with Graeme Jensen and Victor Peirce some weeks prior to the shootings. They didn't end up doing that job and pulled out at the last minute.

Houghton had also been involved along with Peter McEvoy and Peirce in at least two armed hold ups. One was the Newmarket Branch of the State Bank on 12 November 1987 and the second was the Oak Park Branch of the State Bank on 31 March 1988.

Houghton had fired a shotgun blast during that second stick up and it turned out the shotgun he used ended up being the murder weapon at Walsh Street in October that year.

Witness X would later identify Houghton, Peirce and McEvoy from bank photographs she was shown when she came into Witness Protection on 13 July 1989.

After the shootings, Houghton had gone to ground and was proving difficult to locate. He had been under surveillance for a couple of weeks around the early part of November 1988. He had been followed to Bendigo and the covert surveillance teams spent weeks keeping up with and trying to second guess where he was going and what he was doing.

Task Force detectives, including myself, were in Bendigo for a good deal of this time and when it came time to close the net and catch our crook, we were Johnny on the spot.

Houghton had been let run to see if he would lead us to anything that may provide evidence against him and his accomplices.

At this stage, we had not identified the murder weapon and we still didn't have the police revolver taken during the murders. Unfortunately, we still don't have the revolver.

Houghton had met and befriended Paul Widdicombe, a resident of the Bendigo suburb of Long Gully. Widdicombe was married with a couple of children and was in awe of Houghton, having suspected he was involved in crime without specifically knowing what.

He had met Graeme Jensen first through someone he had been in jail with and their first meeting was around the middle of 1987.

Jensen actually introduced Jedd Houghton to Paul Widdicombe, and they went to his house in Sparrowhawk Road on numerous occasions prior to October 1988.

Most of these trips were shooting trips and Widdicombe sourced and purchased ammunition for Houghton's pistols and for shotguns.

It was on one of their shooting trips that Widdicombe introduced the pair to the brand of shotgun ammunition that would later be used with the KTG shotgun at Walsh Street.

Widdicombe had taken Jensen and Houghton out around Bendigo on one of their shooting trips and during the course of that he happened to do a demonstration on a barbeque plate that was lying around in one of the paddocks. The shotgun shell hit the barbeque plate and around three of the pellets penetrated it. This proved fascinating for all involved and that brand of shell then became the preferred load for their shotgun.

After Jensen's death, Houghton called Widdicombe and asked him to go around to his father's place, which was close to Widdicombe's, and let him know that Jensen had been shot dead by the police.

Widdicombe told me he was scared at this stage and although he would not personally go to see Houghton's dad, he did call him on the phone and pass on the message. While he was speaking to Houghton's old man on the phone, he warned Widdicombe to be careful around Jedd as he was a mad bastard when he went off. He told him to stay out of Jedd's way if he 'went silly'. He told Widdicombe that Jedd was 'virtually uncontrollable once he blew his top'. This further reinforced to a now very nervous Widdicombe that Houghton was going to be a problem and potential risk for him and his wife and kids.

So when Houghton appeared not long after the Walsh Street murders, he arrived with his girlfriend Kim Cameron. He left her with Widdicombe and made a couple of trips back and forth from Melbourne. He was by this stage under surveillance by a large team of 'dogs' from the Bureau of Criminal Intelligence (BCI). They had to be very careful when tailing Houghton, as he was pretty switched on when it came to being followed. They managed to keep a relatively close watch on him and as we had the addresses of those close to him, we were able to let him run at times and pick him up by covering the addresses he frequented.

Houghton ended up with Widdicombe at his house before moving to a cabin at the Ascot Lodge Caravan Park in White Cliffs, a suburb of Bendigo. The dogs followed Houghton and Cameron to the location and were able to set up an observation post in one of the nearby cabins.

On the evening of 16 November, Houghton and Cameron took off from the cabin and were kept under surveillance. This gave us the chance to check out their cabin and familiarise ourselves with the layout, should we have to carry out a raid on Houghton. We got a spare key from the bloke who ran the park and a couple of the Task Force detectives and one or two of the dogs went through the cabin. They had to be careful not to move anything or leave any signs that the cabin had been inspected. They got in and out without being caught by anyone and were well out by the time Widdicombe and Cameron returned.

They got back and were 'put to bed' by the observation post crew. Put to bed meant that they were watched constantly until the lights were out and it was obvious they had retired for the night.

At the crack of dawn on the morning of 17 November 1988, Houghton was up and about and off on his way to Widdicombe's house.

While at the house Houghton was mucking around with a scanner that he used to listen to the police radio frequency, trying to keep track should anything come over the airwaves about him. That particular morning he thought the lack of chatter by the police on the radio could mean bad tidings for him and he asked Widdicombe to take him for a drive around the bush outskirts of Bendigo.

At about 7am he got Widdicombe to call his wife Donna from a public phone booth to make sure it was OK to return. Houghton was paranoid and didn't want to walk into a trap, in case we had raided the house and were waiting for him. When Donna answered the phone and was obviously just woken up, Houghton relaxed a little and they felt safe to return. When they got there Houghton continued listening to the scanner and it was his paranoia that'd actually gave him the heads up he was looking for.

While he was playing with the scanner he heard birds singing and a dog barking and thought these sounds were coming through clearer on the scanner. He told Widdicombe to listen to the scanner while he checked around the outside of the house. He was walking around rambling with constant chatter when Widdicombe yelled to him that he was coming through loud and clear on the scanner. Houghton checked around that area and found a wire running from a power source under the house to a window frame. He disconnected the wire from the battery and told Widdicombe what he had found. That was one of our covert listening devices and what a time for him to find it. Now he had taken the advantage and we were reacting to him which made everything much more dangerous, not to mention time critical.

He said, 'They're not going to do what they did to Graeme to me without me putting up a fight'. With that Houghton marched out to Widdicombe's shed and removed three more pistols from a bag he had hidden there earlier. He checked them and made sure they were all loaded and ready to rock and roll should that course of action be required. That made a total of four firearms on Houghton which were loaded and ready for bear. He had one .357 revolver, a 38 calibre revolver and his original two, which from memory I think were around 25 calibre size.

When we were told that he had found the listening device, we were scrambled and made preparations to raid Widdicombe's if required. We were briefed by John Noonan on what was going to happen and were discussing the possibility of raiding Widdicombe's when we were told by the dogs that Houghton was on the move. He left Widdicombe's and went straight back to the cabin at Ascot Lodge and re-joined Cameron, who had stayed there, presumably asleep when Houghton had left at sparrow fart that morning.

Once he was back at the cabin and we knew he was loaded to the teeth and was obviously mad as a cut snake, we knew we could not let him run any longer. We had gone to great pains to keep our presence in Bendigo from Houghton. Now that he had blown our veil of invisibility away, we had to move and move quick. Numerous options were discussed and it was decided it would be safest to try and take him in the cabin.

Once Houghton was back at the cabin, John held an in depth briefing on how we would do the raid. He made application over the phone to have the SOG authorised to do the raid and this was initially denied. We could not believe it. They knew this bloke was most likely one of the shooters from Walsh Street. They were told he had found our listening device and told us he wouldn't go easy and basically come and get him. They knew he was armed with numerous firearms and was extremely agitated and probably the most dangerous he had ever been. It did not seem to matter. The braid refused to use the SOG. So the plans were firmed up for us to carry out the raid. It was this briefing that made me wake up and smell the flowers. We were all wired at the possibility of carrying out the raid and we knew what Houghton had said prior to the device being disconnected.

Isn't it funny what you remember and when? I remember one of the other senior detectives lying on the bed in the motel before the briefing, wearing some flash looking red or maroon sort of smoking jacket. He was propped on the bed reading the newspaper. He reminded me of Hugh Heffner and comments were made as to his attire. He didn't give a rat's arse and thought he looked quite dignified. Which of course he did. Quite the gentleman detective.

The heart was pounding and the adrenaline levels were through the roof as we sat there and listened to my brother. John said either Jim O'Brien or Col Ryan were to do the door. That meant whoever it was would smash the glass cabin door and initiate the breach.

Then he said, 'Joe. You go in first with the shotgun.'

He went on to instruct other Task Force detectives to come in after me, in whatever order it was decided on.

I must admit I lost track of what he said after I heard I was to be first in with the shotty. I nearly forgot to breathe. I thought to myself that I was in real strife here and this was going to be the hairiest raid I'd done, and we'd done plenty since Walsh Street, on some very dangerous crooks. It makes a difference when you know the bloke you're going after is loaded up to buggery and has every intention of shooting it out with us.

After the briefing I waited until my brother was alone before approaching him. I asked him what the bloody hell he was doing. I asked what the story was sending me in first when there was a fair chance I would be shot. He looked straight at me and told me he could not look like he was looking after me or showing me favouritism and so that was why I was to go in first. I thought good one. Fair enough you didn't have to do me any favours, but you didn't have to get me shot either. I was going to pull rank and get him in all sorts of trouble. Then I thought no, going to mum and dad would have been out of line.

I could not say anything more and had to shut up and get myself ready. We had already donned our bullet proof vests and I must say it was the first time I had ever really prayed that these things would actually do what they were supposed to. I checked my 38 calibre revolver with a 4 inch barrel. I liked the longer weapon and had used the same type of long barrelled revolver at the Majors. I liked the greater accuracy and I've no doubt that I liked the thought of carrying as large a firearm as I could. I used to wear it in a shoulder holster that hung down under my arm beneath whatever jacket I had on. It was only during really hot days that I swapped for a snub nose 38 which I'd carry in an ankle holster. That was only because it was too bloody hot having to wear a jacket during summer to keep the weapon hidden from view.

I checked and double checked the Remington 870 shotgun that was the weapon of choice for the squads. I cannot recall whether I had the full stock shotgun or the pistol grip, as we had both on offer at the time. I had done the Tactical Shotgun Course at the Major Crime and this was great to learn how to load on the run and maintain continuous fire during the training. From memory the Remington 870 could hold one shell up the spout and five in the magazine under the barrel. During the training we were taught how to reload and fire it. That entailed holding a shogun shell in your left hand which was used to steady the weapon and the right hand was then used on the trigger mechanism. So the idea was that as you fired the six shells, you could then roll another shell along the fingers of the left hand straight into the firing chamber and so keep loading and firing in a hot swap scenario.

I sat there next to Billy Panagiotaros and Jeff Calderbank and none of us had to say what we were thinking. We all knew this was going to be the most dangerous job we had ever and probably would ever do. I smoked one after the other as we sat around in our vests all tooled up and waiting for the go ahead. I don't know how long we stayed like that but I am of the opinion it was at least an hour or more. Now I had some understanding of how men at war felt when they were waiting to go into battle. It was somehow exhilarating but at the same time it makes you ponder your mortality and you think through God knows how many scenarios of what could or would happen during the raid. All these thoughts plough through your head while at the same time you have to maintain your composure and make sure your gear was ready to go when needed.

After what seemed like hours, we got word that the SOG had been approved and they were on their way. Thank God. I remember the feeling of relief that I was off the hook. There was also a feeling that I had been robbed of a chance at testing myself in the ultimate arena. I am pretty sure the feeling of relief outdid the chance to test myself. These may sound like stupid things to have going through your head, but that's how I felt and what I thought.

Within half an hour or so the SOG flew into the nearest airfield on a small passenger plane. I remember watching them disembark in their blacks, with their kit bags slung either over their shoulders or carried at full stretch in one hand. They were an awe-inspiring sight and I almost wanted to clap and cheer them as they walked from the plane.

As most police were in those days encouraged to be strictly homophobic, that was never really going to happen. I had to settle for my heart clapping and cheering silently on the inside. No high fives. No man hugs. None of that crap had been invented yet. Toughen up princess!

These blokes were the best of the best. They were well drilled, well equipped and professional blokes who were tough as nails and knew their stuff. Except maybe only when they were on the turps and would try and beat the crap out of each other for little or no reason.

I watched them assemble and John Noonan gave their boss the briefing. They all then started to tool up and spread out to unload their kit bags and check weapons.

I remember watching quietly as Kerry McNamara removed his machine pistol of whatever variety and he then appeared to fumble with loading the magazine. He tried three or four times and couldn't get it in. I looked at Billy Panagiotaros as much as to say, 'What's the go with this bloke?' Kerry looked up and saw me looking at Bill and then gave us a smile and without looking picked up the magazine and the weapon and loaded it with one hand without taking his eyes off me. Then the light came on. He had been taking the piss out of us and was never in any trouble loading the weapon. I smiled like an idiot and thought what a cheeky bastard he was before admiring the skill and familiarity he had with his tools of trade. I used to be able to hold a beer in one hand and take out a packet of smokes with the other and remove a smoke with the same hand and light it. I cannot remember, but I don't think my drinking and smoking skills were ever needed at the SOG.

The SOG were always shrouded in an air of invincibility and their arrival on this occasion was no different. Tony Currie and Paul Carr led the assault on Houghton's cabin and even though they had all the specialist gear for the forced entry, they still had dramas as they entered. Houghton had fitted a bar of some description across the glass door. So the SOG went to ream the door with a long baton that would firstly penetrate the glass and then in a circular motion take out the surrounding glass. The entry team would then walk or roll in through the door with weapons at the ready. When they did this they came up against this bar impeding their entry. It cost them precious seconds and gave time for Houghton to grab one of the five weapons he had in the cabin and level one at the entry team.

He was called on to drop the weapon and instead continued to raise it at the SOG.

That was the last thought that went through his head.

The last thing that went through his chest, was a solid slug from a shotgun that stopped his attempted resistance dead in its tracks. He fell slumped on the cabin bed and his girlfriend Kim Cameron was arrested and secured before being removed from the cabin. She was extremely upset, as one would expect.

It gets me how these girls get in with these bad boys and get some sort of thrill from a 'Bonnie and Clyde' experience. She knew or was pretty sure Houghton was an armed robber and had committed the Walsh Street murders. Yet when he gets shot while armed with five weapons that she would have seen him carrying and positioning on himself and in the cabin, she cried foul. She would later allege that Houghton was murdered and that he was never given a chance. I think her father Bill Cameron knew the story would not have a happy ending and I'd bet that he'd rather Kim hadn't gone with this bloke in the first place. He would later relate how Houghton had told him how deep his feelings were for Graeme Jensen before telling him that he had carried out the Walsh Street murders. This was a couple of days before he was shot, when he had gone to Melbourne and visited the parents of his girlfriend. Being a father of a couple of daughters, I often dread what sort of blokes they will go out with. I know one thing for sure, they would not go out with any armed robbing scumbag like Houghton, whether I had anything to do with it or not. If I was in his shoes, Kim Cameron would never have left with Houghton at all.

As soon as the decision was made and the SOG were approved and in place we were switched to the secondary target being Paul Widdicombe's house. We knew he had given sanctuary to Houghton and that he knew what he'd done and the fact that a listening device was found at his house that morning. We knew he had weapons and we did not know how bad he was. So in that circumstance we had to prepare for the worst and moved out to his address.

As soon as we had confirmation that the SOG was a go on Houghton, we simultaneously hit Widdicombe. We had Jeff Calderbank, Bill Panagiotaros, Dave Brodie and I'm pretty sure Fiona Richardson was also there during the raid. I know Steve

Briner, Mark Dog Davis and Peter Two Dogs McCarthy from the
task force intelligence section were also in Bendigo and I can't
remember which of them accompanied us on the raid.

We screamed to the front of Widdicombe's house and flew
out of the blocks as soon as the wheels stopped. The front door
was crashed in by Jeff Calderbank and I barrelled in first with the
shotgun. I was followed by Bill and Dave and the others. As we
came in the door, I saw Donna Widdicombe and one of the kids in
the lounge along with an older woman who I believe was one of
their mothers. As we entered, we were screaming, 'Police. Everyone
get on the ground.'

The Widdicombe house was not a big one and the front door
led to a skinny hallway the opened onto the lounge room in the
middle of the house. Then another door at the end of the lounge
led through to the kitchen at the rear of the house where another
door led to the backyard and the shed. The bedrooms were set at
the front and on one side of the house near then front, as far as I
can remember.

As I went running through the house screaming for everyone
to get down, I saw Paul Widdicombe scramble and make a run
for the door at the end of the lounge. The mother stood there in
shock and didn't know what to do. I ran past her and went after
Widdicombe. As I got near the door, Donna Widdicombe jumped
in front of me and I pushed her into a chair and continued on
after her husband. She was obviously trying to slow my progress
and give her husband time to get out. She didn't realise we had
police covering the rear door as well. So after I brushed her off,
I ran through into the kitchen. I was caught off guard by Paul
Widdicombe rushing at me from near the rear of the door and he
grabbed hold of my shotgun and was trying to take it from me.
I realised what was happening and knew there was no way I was

giving up my weapon. I stopped his charge and started pushing him backward, by pushing the shotgun longways across his chest. I was keeping watch of the trigger to make sure I kept his finger out to prevent him firing the round that was up the spout. I pushed him back into the kitchen sink area and he was leaning over a stack of dishes on the sideboard near the sink. He managed to slip out sideways and reversed our positions. I had my back into the dishes and he was pushing me harder into them, which caused them to be thrown off the sink and onto the floor. Some smashed where they were, and others smashed when they hit the floor of the kitchen.

Then in a classic move straight out of a movie, we somehow went crashing onto the kitchen table and I was wiping whatever was on the table with Widdicombe, who was on his back and was still maintaining his death grip on my shotgun. It was like an ad for cleaning cloths and he was the cloth.

My adrenalin was at full pump and I knew I was fighting for control of that shotgun. I knew if I lost it, I was in more shit than a Werribee duck. This provided me with the requisite motivation to fight like my life depended on it. Without wanting to seem melodramatic it probably did. And that adds even more grit and danger to the story.

After I had cleared the table with his body, I slid him off the table and he hit the floor on his back with me landing on top of him. I was yelling at him to let go of the shotgun, whilst pushing it down across his throat in an attempt to strangle him.

As we rolled and fought, in came Bill Panagiotaros and Dave Brodie who joined in the fray and we fought to overpower Widdicombe. I must say he put up a hell of a fight and was throwing his fists around and going like a thrashing machine. He scored one right on the button and that took the wind out of my sparring partner's sails.

Widdicombe was handcuffed and securely restrained on the floor. I sat there with my back against the cupboard under the kitchen sink and was bathed in sweat and taking big breaths.

This was only one battle waged that day and I must say at the end of it, I had the good guys leading two nil. It was not easy and it was a day of high drama, lots of contemplation and more adrenalin used than I'd ever imagined.

We searched the Widdicombe household and took possession of various items that would help fill in some of the gaps we had in our investigation. The best was the information about the ammunition and the barbeque plate that led us to the origins of the ammo used at Walsh Street.

Widdicombe turned out to be a central figure in the gathering of intelligence on a number of the main players leading up to Walsh Street. He was a simple country boy who got sucked in by the romance of hanging around with what he knew were serious crooks. He knew Houghton had been involved in Walsh Street. He still provided sanctuary to him and gave him knowledge regarding firearms that he didn't possess before he met him. He was instrumental in Houghton using the KTG shotgun with the most damaging ammo and should shoulder some relayed responsibility for the death of two young policemen.

I think it took Houghton's death to temper the romanticism of their little adventure. Houghton lived by the sword and died by the sword. He was a vicious armed robber and killer who had no qualms about shooting two innocent young coppers in cold blood. He never gave them a chance and he ended up against a team of blokes who gave him more opportunity than he had given. He chose his lot and as far as I am concerned he got his right whack.

We ended up taking the statement from Paul Widdicombe and didn't finish until 9 or 10 that night. We had been working huge hours and with the flow of adrenalin and a healthy dose of self-preservation in the form of fear made for a potent mix.

CHAPTER TWENTY

The Gary Abdullah Shooting

Gary Abdullah was more a person of interest more than a suspect in the Walsh Street murders and had been named during early days of the investigation.

In 1988 Abdullah was a 24-year-old father of a six-year-old son to his on again off again girlfriend of many years Christine Angwin. He was a good-looking young bloke and was no doubt popular with the fairer sex.

He had been in youth detention centres as a kid and at 24 had convictions for car theft, assault, burglary and robbery, as well as being suspected of armed robberies. Whether he had been involved in Walsh Street is still questionable and only those involved know for sure.

Jason was the nephew of the prime suspect Victor Peirce and was by now in Witness Protection, having flipped on his family and nominated Abdullah in one of his earliest statements as having supplied a getaway car used in the murders. He had changed his story numerous times and this clouded the veracity of his evidence. There was a fair deal of circumstantial evidence that led the Task Force to believe he had some input, but what his involvement was and still isn't known for sure.

Abdullah was part of the Flemington Crew and was a suspect in numerous armed robberies either as a participant or having supplied vehicles. The gang of suspected armed robbers was believed to include Graeme Jensen, Victor Peirce, Frank Valastro, Mark Militano, Jedd Houghton and Peter McEvoy. Victor Peirce and his stepbrother Trevor Pettingill, along with Peter McEvoy and another mate of Jason's, Anthony Farrell, were later charged with the murders of Constables Tynan and Eyre. There was also strong links to Jason and Mark Moran as well as a crook who in my opinion turned out to have played a pivotal role in the end game, Santo Mercuri.

As at the time of writing, the only member of the Flemington Crew alive is Peter McEvoy. He mouthed off in April 2010 to New South Wales police after being arrested that the sweetest sound he had heard was the pleading of one of the young constables in Walsh Street South Yarra. When I read this, I couldn't believe this mutant was still alive. I knew he had spent most of his life after getting out of jail in hiding, as he was supposedly scared he would be killed by police.

Forensic evidence proved the KTG Shotgun used at Walsh Street was the same weapon used on 31 March 1988 during a botched hold up on the State Bank at Oak Park. Security screens were activated that day and three shots were fired using the shotgun to try and blow the locks off the bank security access door. Their attempts were unsuccessful and they left empty handed. This weapon was believed to have been stolen by Abdullah during a burglary at Rob Reid's Sports Store in Mount Alexander Road, Moonee Ponds on 8 July 1987.

There were actually two of the same KTG brand and two used trade in shotguns stolen during the burglary, with one turning up in the possession of a crook by the name of Michael Hall in about October 1987. Hall claimed he had stolen the sawn off KTG shotgun from Christine Angwin's flat in May Street North Fitzroy when he had broken into it after he went to see her and she wasn't home. Once inside her flat, he had stolen a couple of thousand in cash, a bag of marijuana among other property and then he hit the jackpot. Under her bed he found one of the two stolen KTG shotguns and a white fabric ANZ Bank bag full of $100 notes totalling approximately $8,000.

This information was not ascertained until early 1989, after exhaustive and quite brilliant detective work by Detective Sergeant Peter Signorotto. Siggy was and still is a great bloke and he was known by the troops at the Armed Robbery Squad and the task force as a gun enthusiast and was considered an expert in firearms. He was able to identify the brand of shotgun from photographs of a weapon used during the Oak Park Bank hold up.

It was finally ascertained that of all 42 KTG brand shotguns imported into Australia around 1986, two had been found with some form of circumstantial connection to Gary Abdullah. The sawn off KTG found in Hall's possession had been seized and destroyed by police after his arrest and the other was later ascertained to be the weapon used at the Oak Park hold up and most importantly was the shotgun used at Walsh Street. Whether Abdullah had been on the end of the sawn off KTG Shotgun during the hold up or the murders again no one knows positively.

The second KTG shotgun, and the Walsh Street murder weapon, was found in a garden bed at the Royal Park Golf Course in June 1989. It was dug up by a gardener, wrapped in a green plastic garbage bag. It was rusted on the outside but forensic testing of the inside of the barrel was able to prove it categorically as the murder weapon.

Jeff Calderbank, Bill Panagiotaros and I again drew the short straw and we got to sit off the site of the find in an unmarked car for the night. There had been a media release stating that the weapon had been found but no location was given.

It was hoped the media release might lead to one of the offenders returning to the site to check if it was still where they had buried it at some stage after the Walsh Street murders. I remember we were already knackered from months of long hours and we had to sit in the car and try and stay awake all night in the hope someone would come and check to see if the shotgun mentioned on the news was the same one they buried. No one arrived and we took it in shifts of two being awake and one getting some sleep all through the night and into the late morning. With Geoff Calderbank measuring about 6'4", Billy Panagiotaros around the 6'1" mark and me being Collingwood six-footer, spending the night in any car wasn't ideal. I spent most of the night listening to Bill snoring so loud I had to keep waking him up before he sucked the windows in on the car and left us further exposed to the elements. I have no idea how his wife Helen has stayed with him for the forty something years they have been together. She either suffers from some form of hearing impairment or sleeps at the other end of the house. Geoff was in the back and at times had his legs stretched into the front of the cabin through the gap in the seats. When Bill or I would complain he would nail us with the trials of being so tall and the severity of the space restrictions he was being made to endure. Unfortunately, no one turned up and we had to return to the office and continue on with our other investigations.

From the start Gary Abdullah had been of interest and we spent a great deal of time and effort trying to locate him after Walsh Street. He had stayed in hiding and we knew he was being visited by Christine Angwin on a regular basis. We just didn't know where.

Abdullah had gone deeper to ground after his best mate Jedd Houghton was shot on 17 November 1988 by the Special

Operations Group during a raid on the cabin he was staying in at Bendigo.

As previously mentioned, this shooting created a fair degree of controversy among numerous crooks, especially those aligned to or associated with the Flemington Crew. There had been claims that the SOG shot Houghton dead as a payback for Walsh Street. The investigations made with the Angwins highlighted the problems we had on the Task Force. After the shooting deaths of Mark Militano and Frank Valastro in the lead up to the Jensen shooting, the Flemington community were questioning police and particularly the Armed Robbery Squad on their conduct. This community was overwhelmingly comprised of low-income earners with a major reliance on social welfare and public housing, as evidenced by the monolithic housing commission towers that were prevalent in the Flemington and surrounding areas. The housing commission flats were either walk ups or high rise. The walk ups were around three or six stories and the high rise were anywhere from 18 to 20 floors. The housing commission flats were most definitely devoid of character as they were bastards to have to go into. We used to get in the elevators at some of these places and if we were spotted, which was most of the time, one of the less community minded tenants would either urinate or defecate in the lift before we got in. Imagine being an elderly pensioner sharing these lifts with some of these shitheads. What a way to live.

The Civil Libertarians suggested it would have been very difficult to have any confidence or trust in the police force as a whole during these times and this animosity and mistrust spread to all corners of the criminal community. These local communities operated under a siege mentality and it made for good glue to bond them strongly together against their common enemy: the police. It made our task of trying to illicit intelligence and cooperation almost impossible. I have never been involved with such a tight knit and unified group. No one provided any assistance no matter the threat of prosecution or inducement to tell what they knew.

Surveillance around the housing commission flats of Flemington, Carlton and many other inner-city suburbs proved almost impossible as well. The people we wanted to speak to, their families and friends, held the high ground. They could look over their balconies and see approaching police cars and foot traffic and had plenty of time to provide a warning and arrange hiding places for their mates. They had an uncanny knack of spotting covert surveillance and at times it was quite disconcerting how they could identify complete teams of undercover police and their vehicles.

We had many premises utilised as observations posts and had plain clothes police occupying vacant commission flats at times trying to man these posts. It was particularly difficult and required the two person crews manning the Observation Posts (Ops) to work on 24-hour shifts to try and minimise the comings and goings of too many people that were not known at the flats. Their underground network of intelligence spotters was comprehensive to say the least. It proved to be very dangerous times for our covert criminal intelligence operatives and technicians. Some of the sites they had to try and get into, place listening device and telephone intercepts and get out without being seen were hair raising. If they had been caught by some of the people we were trying to bug, they would have been in serious trouble. I get antsy enough even today watching actors try and do it during movies let alone in real life.

The areas of interest for us were proving impossible to penetrate. The shooting death of Gary Abdullah in April 1989 lit the fuse of public outrage that had been up to that point, centred around dead armed robbery suspects and hardened criminals. Abdullah was allegedly being told by all and sundry that Task Force detectives were going to kill him. We were not spreading this rumour and we definitely didn't want him dead. Whether we loved or loathed him, he was of no evidentiary value to us dead. If he was involved in any way, we wanted to know how, when, where, why and with whom.

During the months after October 1988 there were numerous raids on suspects and associates of suspects. Abdullah was no different.

On 6 December 1988 there were a large number of coordinated raids carried out on suspects and their family and associates. Some very heavy crooks were turned upside down that day and we had an incredibly successful day. We found drugs, firearms and various other property in the possession of some of the most notorious crooks in Victoria. Unfortunately, we did not find any physical evidence or ascertain any intelligence to link anyone to Walsh Street. The good side for us was that the state's criminal fraternity were more than aware that this conduct would continue until we got what we wanted.

We spent a great deal of time going back to see friends, family and associates of Abdullah during the early part of 1989. We had heard the rumours that people had been told that we were going to kill Abdullah if we found him. It was decided that the best way to fix this misconception was to go back and let them know that it was not members of the Task Force that had been spreading this rumour. It did not make our job any easier and we had to deal with the mistrust of everyone we spoke to.

We left messages for Abdullah to contact us to clear the matter up. In the siege mentality they lived within, any show of cooperation for our investigation would have been viewed by their 'society' as collaboration. To my way of thinking, you co-operate with friends and you collaborate with the enemy. And we were most assuredly viewed as the enemy.

Finally, on 22 February 1989 Gary Abdullah came into the St Kilda Road Police Complex in the company of his solicitor, Bruno Kiernan. Kiernan had been asked by Abdullah to make an appointment with my brother and he did just that. When he came in that day, Abdullah was spoken to in his presence. John Noonan explained the state of play honestly to Abdullah. He told him how there had been mention of the involvement of a 'Gary from the Carlton Flats'. He told him this person had been alleged to have supplied a car and he asked him if he had any involvement in the Walsh Street murders.

John told us that day it was a frank and open discussion where Abdullah was asked if he was involved and told that unless he said otherwise, we did not believe he was. Abdullah said he did not know where he was on the night preceding Walsh Street and denied having received any phone calls from any of the people suspected of committing the murders. He told John that he had sold his Gemini sedan before the murders and definitely had not been involved in supplying a car at any stage.

After their conversation, Abdullah was taken to the Arson Squad and interviewed and charged with setting fire at Simon's Disco in Northcote. He was bailed and left the building some hours later.

Even though Abdullah had said he was not involved, John wanted him followed and had organised surveillance crews to pick him up as he left St Kilda Road. This happened, but unbelievably he lost them and threw the tail in a matter of minutes. We could not believe it. How the bloody hell could he throw the tail that quick? Unfortunately, these blokes were so switched on to being followed that it was a big ask to expect our surveillance teams to keep track of him. That was the fact, but I remember at the time

everyone concerned was more than pissed off at how quickly he
had lost them.

At least as a result of talking to him, we learned that he was
renting a flat in Drummond Street, North Carlton. Covert
surveillance technicians managed to get in and plant listening
devices and a telephone intercept was approved. A listening post
was set up in the school opposite the block of flats and was manned
by police from the Task Force Special Projects Unit, which was
always abbreviated to the rather unsavoury SPU Crew, who were
tasked with this function throughout the investigation.

It's been mentioned on numerous occasions that it was strange
that after speaking to Abdullah and him assuring us that he wasn't
involved, that we would then spend so much time and resource in
bugging his flat and tapping his phones. I know everyone might
have been expecting he was given a hug and left as friends when
he was spoken to by my brother and denied his involvement.
If everyone who denied their involvement in crime were not
investigated further, there would not be many crimes solved. It does
not happen like in the police shows, where everything is wrapped
up in the course of an hour including ads. It's like the sales process.
It usually only starts when the prospect says no.

Abdullah didn't do or say anything that we hadn't expected
him to say or do. He denied being involved in the murders of
two policemen. I doubt whether anyone would have thrown their
hands up and used the old 'you got me' routine before confessing.
We had to play this hand out and the only way to prove or disprove
his involvement in any capacity in Walsh Street was to continue to
monitor him to see if he said or did anything that could assist our
investigation. Even if he weren't involved, that doesn't mean that he
could not have been of assistance. He was in the Flemington Crew
and was friends with most of the main suspects for Walsh Street.

He might have been told something of interest on the phone or in conversations at his flat with anyone who was involved in the murders. To think we would have just taken his word for it and let him go without any further investigation would be naïve. It would have also been tantamount to dereliction of duty and would have done nothing to further our cause.

The surveillance and listening to Abdullah continued twenty-four hours a day, seven days a week. Then in early March 1989, Abdullah came to the fore again. He was allegedly involved in trying to kill someone out the front of a nightclub in King Street Melbourne. As it turned out, he saw an argument between a girlfriend he was with and a young bloke near a hotdog van. It ended with his girlfriend screaming abuse at the bloke before Abdullah sparked up his mum's car and ran over the young nightclub patron. From memory he also reversed over him. He was obviously trying to do the bloke serious harm, if not kill him and it showed that the good-looking baby-faced Gary Abdullah could be a cold and calculating prick. He should have killed that young bloke that night and he was bloody lucky he didn't. As it turned out, he was the son of a police detective in the western suburbs of Melbourne and this enquiry was conducted by the local City West CIB personnel.

On Sunday 9 April 1989 I was working at the Task Force offices still transcribing listening device tapes, along with Bill Panagiotaros and Geoff Calderbank. We were in the communications room, as this was where we had all the tape transcription machines set up. At about 3pm we received a call from D24 that City West detectives had spotted Gary Abdullah at his flat in Drummond Street Carlton. I spoke to the operator at D24 and relayed the message from Calderbank to the City West Detectives. 'Do not attempt to arrest Abdullah until we get there.'

The three of us ran down to the car park and drove like mad men out to Carlton from St Kilda Road. It did not take us long and we got there in less than 10 minutes and came to a sudden halt out the front of the block of flats. We did not drive into the block of flats because we weren't able to ascertain what was happening, as there'd been no response to our numerous calls to the City West detectives via D24. We parked in the street and walked down the driveway. I saw Senior Detective Cliff Lockwood come walking out of the stairwell onto the driveway. He looked stoned. He was swaggering and looked like he had seen a ghost. Little did I know he had done his best to create one!

I approached Lockwood and he looked at me and said, 'I shot him.'

I asked where he was and he said he was in the flat upstairs and pointed away at the stairwell leading up to the flat. Bill and I ran up the stairs and into the flat on the first floor. When we entered the flat I noticed it was empty. There wasn't any furniture and it looked as if it had been vacated. We looked around the flat and I saw Senior Detective Dermot Avon in the back bedroom with the prone body of Gary Abdullah.

On entering the flat and particularly the room, there was the strong smell of gunpowder and it didn't take Einstein to work out there had been shots fired. As I walked in, Senior Detective Dermot Avon, who was working with Lockwood, was crouched over Abdullah and he was giving him mouth to mouth resuscitation.

I said G'day to Dermot and he looked up at me with what I would best describe as a terrified look on his face. He looked deeply upset and to me appeared to be teetering on the brink of tears. Dermot Avon is a very big bloke and was doing his best to keep working on Abdullah, which I found interesting. I said to him to give it a break and go downstairs and I would take over the CPR.

Dermot took what seemed to me to be a long time to comprehend what I was saying and I moved to the opposite side of Abdullah and checked for a pulse. I couldn't find one and started to give him chest compressions.

Dermot stood and moved away from Abdullah and looked at me working on him. I again asked him to go downstairs and wait for the ambulance. I didn't know who had fired the shots and I wanted to get Avon out of the room and away from the scene as soon as possible. He registered what I had said and walked from the room.

Billy Panagiotaros went downstairs with Dermot and stayed with him, Jeff Calderbank and Cliff Lockwood. I asked Bill to give me a yell when the ambulance arrived. I remembered when we first walked in we looked at each other and the silent message between the two of us was, 'Oh shit. What's happened here?'

I looked around the room and noticed a large pistol lying on the other side of the prone figure of Abdullah whilst I was trying to concentrate on doing the CPR. I had that much going around in my head and I was trying to remember how many times I was supposed to do compressions before I did mouth to mouth.

As time had slowed down, I got the same feeling I had when I was holding Constable Neil Clinch when he had been shot during a police raid. Abdullah had one eye partially open and the other was open more. He appeared to be looking at me and I didn't know whether he could hear me or not. I could not believe it. Here I was again tending to a young man who had what appeared to me to be fatal gunshot wounds. I wondered whether I should even be doing CPR on someone that may have been part of the murder of Constables Tynan and Eyre. It did pass through my head, that maybe I should stop doing CPR and let him go. I thought what other police would think of me if I saved the life of one of the suspects in a double police murder.

I continued giving him CPR and then stopped and checked his pulse again. I nearly had a heart attack myself. There was a pulse and I honestly felt like I had done something wrong. I must say there was a feeling of relief because I honestly don't know whether I could have given him mouth to mouth. I had also been thinking about that during this time and I was having an internal struggle trying to assess if I would, or in fact could. As luck would have it, I did not have to as he was breathing, although it was shallow. I thought, fuck what I am going to tell the others? I saved Gary Abdullah. I panicked for a few seconds and then thank God I heard Bill yell out as he came up the stairs with the ambulance paramedics. As they entered, I greeted them and moved aside. I told one of the ambos that I had been giving CPR and that he had a pulse again. As one ambo started preparing Abdullah for treatment, the other was unpacking their gear. He looked at Abdullah and said something I cannot remember now. It was then that I thought, Oh shit the listening device is still recording. I did not want the ambulance blokes saying anything that might embarrass them if they ever had to attend court over the shooting. I must say at the time, I was thinking it would be the Coroners Court. I looked at the bloke who made the comment and indicated with my hand that the room had a recording device in it. Both ambulance officers acknowledged and understood what I meant. It was later alleged that I had done this as some part of a conspiracy to cover up for Lockwood and Avon. Nothing was further from the truth. No matter what had happened, there was no need to let blokes who were only doing their best for Abdullah say anything stupid that would be repeated later in court.

While they began working on him, I had a close look at the pistol and realised it was an imitation. I looked more closely around the room and noticed the various blood spatters and bullet holes in the walls. I cannot remember exactly how many there were. But there were enough to make me feel decidedly uncomfortable.

While I was doing CPR on Abdullah, I noticed some of his injuries and asked myself how the hell he would have got them. I'm not going into any more detail of the scene or the injuries, as that would serve no purpose and would only upset people that don't need to be upset any more than what they have been. I did notice a wound to his hand and another to his head that made me question how he would have got them. I was no forensic expert, but I still noticed what I did and felt.

Unbeknownst to me the listening device had been turned off that morning.

I have read recently that the covert surveillance unit was apparently also sitting off Abdullah and saw him intercepted by the City West Detectives. In the book Snouts in the Trough, written by Andrew Fraser on behalf of jailed former drug squad detective Malcolm Rosenes, Rosenes claims that he was part of that surveillance crew and was shocked to have been taken off the surveillance after Abdullah was arrested by the detectives. He claimed it was standard operating procedure to stick around and follow up what happened after apprehension. I do not doubt his concern, but I can guarantee that no one at the Task Force knew what was going to happen and in no way were the surveillance crews called off to remove any potential witnesses. The listening post was shut down that day because we knew his lease was up and as he had not been there for weeks previous. Why would we keep it going? I understand the conspiracy theorists will not be satisfied with some of my answers, but it's the truth. There is no way I would have been involved in the planning, preparation or execution of anyone and I resented the accusation.

When I was called to the inquest as part of the Police Shootings Enquiry by Coroner Hal Hallenstein, I was asked numerous questions by some of the mob of Queens Counsels appearing before the hearing. A top QC asked me several times whether I had conspired with my brother to murder Gary Abdullah. I was shocked at the questioning and it made me angry that I was being asked this. Looking back over thirty years later and taking a more unbiased view of what happened and how it looked, I can understand why I was asked that question. If I was on their side, I would have put two and two together and got five as well.

While we waited for the Homicide Squad to arrive, we started canvassing the flats around Abdullah's looking for any potential witnesses to what might have happened. Jeff Calderbank and I did the door knocks and Bill Panagiotaros maintained the integrity of the scene.

We spoke to the occupants of one of the flats below Abdullah's and asked them if they had heard anything. To my relief one of the two sisters living there said they had heard loud shouting and she assumed it was the police. They both said they heard a male voice yelling out 'drop the gun, drop the gun' or words to that effect. They then heard multiple shots fired one after another and interspersed with the continued calls to drop the weapon. These two young ladies swore black and blue that they had heard was what they heard, and I had no cause to doubt them. We ended taking statements from the two sisters which were subsequently handed to the Homicide Squad on their arrival.

After we finished at the scene we got ready to clear and go back to the office. We had to organise uniform coppers to sit off the address as there were still forensic enquiries to be conducted at the scene. A van crew arrived in the dark and I remember briefing them. I told them to make sure they stayed awake and told them

the circumstances of Walsh Street and the circumstances as we
knew it that afternoon. I reiterated that they could be easy targets
for another reprisal shooting, should they let their guard down
and they confirmed my warnings. They parked their divisional van
near the front driveway and we left the scene after also telling the
two uniform blokes we would be back early the next morning to
relieve them.

We went back to the office and had to take our notes and make
statements on what we had done. Billy Panagiotaros and I headed
back to Drummond Street at around 6am to relieve the van crew.
What I saw on our arrival still haunts me today. The van was parked
where it was the night before and we parked right next to them.
The driver's window was all the way down, as was the passenger
window. Both uniform coppers were slumped in the car and one of
their pistols was clearly visible on the dashboard of the van. For one
terrifying moment I envisaged we had just walked into another
Walsh Street murder scene.

I approached the driver's side window and had my service
revolver unclipped and ready to go. I yelled something to the van
crew and there was no response. I walked to the driver's window
and looked more closely at the two uniform constables and could
not see any blood or evidence of a shooting. I reached in through
the window and took the revolver off the dashboard. I checked it
and saw it was loaded. I then saw the other revolver in the centre
console of the van. I leaned in over the driver and took that
weapon out of the van as well. I also removed their portable police
radio from the centre console.

I poked the driver in the chest and yelled at him to wake up.
He slowly roused and through sleep drowsy eyes he tried to focus
on me and comprehend what was happening. He was looking
around the interior of the van and then outside it like a hung-over
adolescent would on waking from a big night. Bill then poked the
passenger and he came to life a little bit quicker than his driver. I

yelled at them through the window asking what the fuck they were doing. I was filled with a rage that I wasn't used to experiencing. These were two young uniform coppers and they looked younger than Steve Tynan and Damien Eyre were when they were murdered. They were kids and they had fallen asleep. I could not believe that they didn't value their safety and their lives like I did. I was shocked, appalled and mad as a meat axe.

I said, 'Didn't I tell you this bloke may have had some involvement in the murders of two young coppers just like you two?'

They didn't reply but looked at me like I was some form of deranged nut job myself.

I screamed, 'I told you to stay awake. I said there was a fair chance there might be a reprisal shooting like Walsh Street. We get here and you two fucking idiots have got your windows down and are fast asleep. You could've both been killed and with your own guns!'

The driver had gone scarlet and was cranky and made some smart-arse reply about wanting me to stop yelling at them and calm down.

I was beside myself and said, 'Calm down. For fuck's sake. I've got both your weapons and your fucking radio. I could've killed both of you easy and you tell me to fucking calm down!'

He continued to try and argue with me and I screamed at them to shut up and I was going to get onto their boss and have them both charged. I gave them their weapons back after unloading them and handed their radio back as well.

I walked away at the ushering of Bill Panagiotaros, as I think he saw that I had lost it and wasn't in control of myself. I wanted to drag the driver out and punch the shit out of him. I remember thinking to myself, how many police shootings am I going to have to go to before people wise up? I knew one thing for sure. I had seen enough young dead people to do me for a few lifetimes and I didn't want to see anymore. Especially not in uniform.

CHAPTER TWENTY ONE

Airforce One

One lighter moment in my career involved an officer who was colloquially referred to as The Boss. This was usual to call the senior officer 'Boss' as it made him feel important and was a great deal easier than saying his full title. It also saved me from being deferential to someone I did not respect or admire in any way. That line was sponsored by Mick McGann, a former Homicide Squad Detective in NSW. He is a Valour Award winner in NSW and was right in the middle of the Milperra Bikie Massacre. He reckoned he could not bear to salute dickheads and so used boss as a non-committal peace offering.

The Boss was a big bloke, standing over 6'2" tall, and was a solid boy. He had a big barrel chest and a well-developed beer gut, no doubt due to the amount of grog he consumed. He was always gruff and didn't waste a great deal of his time talking to the subordinate ranks such as myself.

The task force had its own offices which consisted of two offices for the Inspectors, a slightly larger open office for the intelligence and computer blokes, of which there were three. Then the rest of us sat in a larger common area with our desks situated all around the room, which nowadays is referred to as open plan.

There was a small office that served as a communications centre, with the police radio base station in there, along with more of the crew who were at this stage transcribing listening device tapes. The transcriptions were done mainly by the task force detectives and some uniform coppers, both male and female, that had also been seconded to the task force.

Out the front of all this was a large meal room which doubled up as our briefing room and could seat twenty odd people if required, which it did on numerous occasions.

On this particular day, I was sitting in the Comms Room with my headset on listening to tape after tape and doing transcriptions of listening device and telephone intercept recordings. They were actual tape recordings in those days as CDs and the rest of the technological advancements had not been invented at that stage. I was working with Sergeant Jeff Calderbank and Billy Panagiotaros. All of us had been bitching and whinging about being knackered and were sick to death of listening to and transcribing those bloody tapes. You might have to listen to the same tape three of four times to confirm what was said by the crooks we were working on. Each tape took on average 90 minutes to listen to and when each one was listened to over and over you can do the maths. Sometimes you would get one of the other people to have a listen to a particular part of a tape, to get their idea on what the crooks were saying. If there was any valuable intelligence gathered, it went straight to the sergeant or one of the inspectors for their thoughts and action, if deemed important enough.

I used to find it amusing that what information we gathered from these degenerate scumbags was called intelligence. They were the worst human beings you would ever come across and some of their monitored conversations would make the hair stand up on the back of my neck. I despised them not just for the crimes they had committed, but because they were almost subhuman in their speech, as well as their demeanour. It has been suggested the best remedy for these people would be controlled breeding. Some people were just bad, and no amount of rehabilitation, empathy, sympathy or intervention would change them. They were scum and they would die scum and no matter what was said or done by any of the plethora of do-gooders to the contrary, it would not change them. One of my favourite sayings was. 'You can put lipstick on a pig. Buts it's still a pig.'

All of a sudden, the door flew open and in walked The Boss. There was no greeting of 'Good morning men' or 'How are you all?', like any civilised gentleman would say on entering a room. He scanned the three of us in the room without acknowledgement and asked, 'Where's Signorotto?'

He was referring to Detective Sergeant Peter Signorotto, who was out of the office doing something or other.

The Boss asked his question to no-one in particular. That was usual, as he thought as soon as he entered the room everyone would give their undivided attention to him, no matter what they were doing.

I took off my headset while Jeff, being the senior member, replied to the question. In that circumstance it was the 'done thing' to defer to your sergeant to answer questions unless they were specifically addressed to you.

He said, 'He's up in the chopper boss.'

'What the fuck's he doing up in the chopper?'

The chopper was the police helicopter and was used to perform aerial surveillance, check out an address that may be going to be raided, or to take aerial photographs for whatever reason.

'I think he is looking at an address,' Jeff replied.

'What address? Why the bloody hell doesn't anyone tell me what they're doing before they do it?'

Again, this tirade was directed to no-one in particular.

'I don't know boss. Would you like me to find out?' Jeff replied.

The Boss looked around the office and his eyes came to rest on the communication base station that sat on its own desk in the corner near the whiteboard. You could see the wheels going around as he thought this might be an opportunity to show us dickheads that he knew how to do things.

He marched over to the base station and snatched the handpiece out of its U-shaped silver holder that was attached to the side of the black box, with LED displays on the front. The LED displayed what channel you were on and whether in fact the unit was turned on.

He pushed the little button on the side of the handpiece and said in his gruff manner, 'VKC this is Crime 100. Over.'

In practical application you would call VKC, identify yourself and wait for a reply. He got no reply and repeated his call. Again, no response. We knew why. It was because the Task Force operated on a special channel that wasn't easy for anyone listening to pick up on a scanner and wasn't on the normal area band that all units in a region used.

The boss looked at all of us and said, 'What the bloody hell's wrong with this bloody thing?'

I kept a straight face and said, 'There's no operator on that channel boss. So just call the unit or ask for Sergeant Signorotto and he should come up.'

He said, 'Crime 100 to Air force one. The unit with Detective Sergeant Signorotto.'

He was visibly angry and no doubt anyone listening to on the radio that day would have picked up on his building frustration. We all looked at each other, as we were behind him, and knew what he had said and were trying not to laugh.

The boss tried the same call a couple of times before throwing the hand piece onto the table and yelling, 'What the bloody hell is wrong with this thing? This shit never works when you need it.'

I started to laugh and turned away so the boss couldn't see me and Bill had done the same. Jeff was stuck looking at us and the boss and could not talk for fear of bursting out laughing as well. I recovered first and thought this would be a great opportunity to embarrass the boss and make him look like the goose he was.

I moved out of my chair towards the radio and said, 'Here boss, let's put it over to Channel 9 and see if you can raise him there.'

The boss snatched the handpiece off me and I thought for a minute he was actually going to thank me. That never happened. Instead he turned back to the radio and got himself composed again to call for Sergeant Signorotto.

Channel 9 was the police channel that covered the entire inner-city suburbs of Melbourne. Every police car in the district would listen to the boss. Perfect. Jeff and Bill both looked at me realising what I had just done and Bill continued laughing in what I would best describe as a covert manner, to use police terminology. Jeff looked at me and could not make up his mind whether he should stop the Boss or let him go. He looked like he did not know whether he was going to laugh or get himself in the shit because of me.

The Boss clicked on the mike and said, 'VKC this is Crime 100 and I'm looking for Air Force One.' He spoke in his deep voice and was trying to sound as authoritarian as he could.

There was a pause and the D24 operator came back saying, 'Could the unit calling VKC please repeat your message. Over.'

Before replying to the operator, he said, 'Fucking idiot. Is he deaf? VKC this is Crime 100 and I am after Air Force One. The chopper with Detective Sergeant Signorotto on board. Over.'

He was getting louder and was speaking in a more pronounced manner. Bill and I were still laughing and struggled with ourselves to keep quiet. Jeff walked away from the boss towards the door and looked at me with a look of 'Good one stupid. We're going to be in deep shit here.'

I gave the 'What did I do?' look back at Jeff and continued to try holding myself together.

After what seemed an eternity but was probably only 20 seconds, the D24 operator replied saying, 'Unit calling the President of the United States?'

We could hear the laughter and derision in his voice when he had responded to the Boss. The Boss was getting fired up now and was going red in the face. He spoke louder again and purposefully began to talk slower and more pronounced. Obviously going to put this smartarse operator in his place for trying to make him look like a fool.

He said, 'VKC this is Crime 100 and I am looking for the helicopter containing Sergeant Signorotto. Did you understand THAT? Over.'

The operator responded with, 'Crime 100, Air Force One is the call sign for the President of the United States. The helicopter from our Air Wing is called sign Air 490. Is that the unit you are after?'

The boss turned and glared at me and I was too scared to laugh and looked back at the boss and said, 'Oh yeah. Sorry Boss. I get these bloody call signs mixed up as well.'

The operator called, 'VKC to Air 490. Unit with Sergeant Signorotto on board.'

Air 490 responded with 'Roger that VKC. We got all that and Sergeant Signorotto will call the office and speak to the boss in about 10 minutes when we land. Over'.

There were no mobile phones in those days, so the landline was the only means of telecommunications available. Laughter could be heard in the background as the pilot of Air 490 made his response.

The D24 operator said, 'VKC to Crime 100. Did you receive the last from Air 490?'

The Boss squeezed the microphone that hard in his big fist that I thought he was going to break it and replied in an angry but controlled response with, 'VKC this is Crime 100. Received. Over and Out.'

He threw the handpiece at the radio set and turned on me and I was looking stone faced back at him, not knowing what the big fellow was going to do. The Boss was as red as a beetroot and his eyes were popping out of their sockets, he was so angry. He knew he had been made to look incompetent in front of not only us but every unit on the road in the area covering most of the city area. Then units started coming up on the radio making smart arse comments hanging shit on the boss. None of them identified themselves and nearly all of their comments with American accents.

The boss burst out with, 'Why the bloody hell I am surrounded by bloody idiots and shit radio gear you have to be a goddam astronaut to fly?'

He stormed out of the office and Jeff, Bill and I all looked at each other and burst out laughing. It was the kind of laughter that you thought you were going to pass out from. We could not breathe and were racked with wave after wave, which had been made worse by the fact that it had been suppressed for so long while the boss had been in the room.

We were all red faced and perspiring by the time we settled down and then every time we just about got ourselves under control, one of us would mention Airforce One and we had burst out again.

I was talking to Bill Panagiotaros the other day and he still mentioned it and laughs at the thought.

CHAPTER TWENTY TWO

The Rental Car Fiasco

One day on the task force near the end of March 1989, I was approached by another officer who again we will simply refer to as The Boss. He marched up to my desk and said without greeting me in any fashion, 'What car have you got?'

I replied, 'One of the hire cars Boss.'

He threw a set of car keys on my desk and said, 'Here take this heap of shit back and get another one.'

The task force had been hiring rental cars because they were unmarked, and the fact of the matter was the police department was under resourced and did not have enough vehicles to go around. An agreement had been made with a local office of a national car rental firm. Officers would regularly come and borrow a car from the task force, knowing we had plenty most of the time and during the day many were available.

I was sitting next to Bill and said to him, 'Hey Billy. Do you want to follow me to the car rental joint so I can change this car over?'

Bill agreed and off we went.

I drove The Boss' car down from the third interior level of the police headquarters building where they were parked. It was a spiral driveway with multiple three-foot-thick concrete columns on the passenger side on the way down that had to be avoided.

I delivered the rental car and spoke to the manager who looked to be a one-man band at the time. The manager said, 'Before you go I better do an inspection and get you to sign it.'

I agreed and walked outside with the manager and his inspection checklist.

He went around the car and stopped on the off or passenger side and said, 'What the bloody hell happened here?'

I walked over to where he was standing and saw the whole side of the car from the front panel to the rear panel, including both doors had been significantly damaged and dented. I replied, 'Mate I didn't even see that. One of the bosses has been driving it and he just told me to bring it back and change it over. He didn't say he'd dinged it.'

He recorded the damage on a picture of a car that he had printed on the checklist and I signed it to acknowledge the damage. I said I would find out what happened when I got back to the office. Bill and I headed back with a new rental car.

On our return to the office, I went and spoke to John Noonan and outlined what the story was with the rental car. John said he would follow it up with The Boss later that day as he was neck deep in problems at that stage and one hire car wasn't going to leapfrog to the top of his list.

Later that day John approached my desk and asked me to come into his office. He said, 'Hey, don't say anything about the rental car. The Boss got pissed and rubbed against one of the pillars in the car park on the way down last night. He's bloody hopeless when he's pissed and he still drives. I asked him if he was going to do accident reports and he said 'fuck 'em. It's only a hire car. So anyway, just keep it quiet and I'll keep an eye on him.'

As if John did not have enough to do running the Task Force without having to babysit these blokes as well. I agreed and that was that. It was not my car and the Boss didn't give a rat's arse, why should I.

Not more than a week later the exact same thing happened. This time I went straight to John before returning the car.

'Is it as bad as the last one?' John said.

'About the same. He's wiped out the passenger side from the front to the back again,' I replied.

'Shit. I'll call the manager at the rental company and you take the car back and change it over. Don't say anything about how it happened. Just tell him you don't know and leave it at that.'

I returned the rental car with Bill again but this time I let him go through the same inspection and grief-stricken reaction of the poor young manager.

Bill got into the car with me and said, 'He's one unhappy bloke. He said he hasn't got another sedan to give us yet but he'll call your brother when he's got one. He reckons he's going to get in all sorts of shit with his boss over this one because he reckons he got his arse chewed out over the first one.'

Bill and I drove back to the Task Force office and filled John in on the story and the reaction.

At the end of that week this particular boss went on leave and took one of the rental cars with him.

John was fuming and said to a gathering of Task Force Detectives over a cup of tea, 'He's unbelievable that bloke. He knows we're short on cars and he goes on leave and takes one of the bloody hire cars with him. I'm not complaining about him going on leave. I wish he would stay on leave. At least that'd be one thing I don't have to worry about all the time and put up with his bullshit.'

The start of the next week soon rolled around. The number of hours everyone was working left little or any time for family, social activities of any kind, or more importantly sleep for everyone involved. After a briefing on the progress of the job everyone went back to what investigations they were doing.

At about 10.30am in strolls the Boss. He was in his suit and tie but looked like he had slept in it or more likely had not had it dry cleaned from when he went on leave. His eyes look like road maps and it appeared to me that he was probably still pissed. He swaggered over to my desk, again with no greeting of any kind and threw another set of car keys onto my blotter.

'Here. Take this heap of shit back to the rental mob and make sure you tell them it's a heap of shit and that I said so,' He said.

He walked off to John's office where he stayed for a short chat before walking out of the office to wherever he went during the day. I sat at my desk looking at the car keys for some time and thought to myself, this is not good. I finally finished my cup of tea like it was going to be my last drink and summoned the courage to go to the lift and down to the car park to inspect the rental car. All the time I was running possible scenarios through my mind of what the car would look like. I tried to look on the bright side and reminded myself what I had been told once by professional motivator Robin Daubeny who said '95% of what you worry about never happens'. I was feeling marginally better having thought a positive thought and watched as the doors of the elevator opened. I walked slowly out and scanned the car park for the matching tag number on the keys. I did not have to look far. I saw what used to be a Sigma sedan parked on an angle across two parking bays, as if to highlight the state it was in. I stopped dead in my tracks and surveyed the scene in front of me.

The car's colour was indiscernible due to the shear amount of caked on mud and dirt. The front windscreen had a crack running from the driver's side to the passenger side. One of the tyres looked half inflated and the rim was bent out of round, obviously from a rather hard impact with some immovable object.

I walked over to the driver's door, unlocked and opened it. I did so like a man trying to take something off a dead body. I was trying not to end up covered in whatever it was that coated the car.

I opened the rear driver's side door as well. I stepped back a few steps in shock and looked at the interior of the car. It was littered with the remnants of beer cans, to the point where you'd struggle to get anyone else bar the driver into the car. The seats were covered in some black slimy shit and finger marks were visible on all instruments, including the rear vision mirror, steering wheel, centre console and seats themselves.

At its peak, the back-bench seat used to be a cloth seat of some description. Now it was coated with a thicker application of the black shit but was complemented with clumps of wool. I touched it and rubbed my fingertips together to spread it and then had a whiff. I didn't put it to my tongue like you see coppers do in the movies. I was 90% sure it was engine oil and that was as far as I was going to go to prove it. I picked up a clump of the wool and looked closer in the rear seat. There was what looked like hoof marks of dirt transposed on top of the layer of oil.

I had seen enough and imagined what my brother was going to say when he saw this. He was going to go off tap and that made me chuckle just a little to myself. It must be a fraternal thing because John normally got his biggest laughs when I hurt myself in some stupid way or made a dick of myself. So when the chance came to reciprocate I always took it, although I also kept a safe distance from him and was careful to judge each facial movement and vocal nuance to know when to flee and when to laugh.

I cautiously closed and locked the doors and returned to the lift well. I reached our floor and went to the toilets to wash my hands of the oil slick, so that I did not inadvertently transfer it onto every surface in the task force office. I also wanted in no way to pre-warn John as to the state of the hire car. I had a different sense of humour and was relishing the reaction I was going to witness from my unsuspecting brother.

I walked into the office and went straight to Jeff Calderbank and told him what I had seen. Together we let out a small conspiratorial laugh and prepared to inform John. We agreed we would not detail what was wrong with the car, but just tell him he would have to see the condition of the car before it was somehow returned. We walked into his office after knocking first, as was only common courtesy. Jeff started and then immediately bailed out and introduced me to provide the details. John looked like he was in the middle of something and was trying to suppress his annoyance at being interrupted.

'You better come and have a look at the rental car the boss has just told me to take back,' I said.

'Look I'm flat out here. Can't you just take care of it?' John asked.

I persisted, 'Not this one. I'm not taking this car back even if it is capable of being driven, which I doubt. You're going to have to handle this one or at least tell us what to say to the poor bastard at the rental car joint.'

'Why, what's he done now?' he said.

'Nothing I say will do it justice. You're going to have to see this for yourself. It's seriously rooted. Inside and out.'

John sat there looking at me to see if I was playing any sort of practical joke on him.

'You better not be buggering around here, I'm telling you. I've got shit loads on. Are you joking or not?' he warned.

I looked straight at him and said, 'Honest to God. You have to see this car or you won't believe it.'

John dropped his pen and said, 'Alright. You two come with me and it better be fair dinkum.'

I led the way as John marched behind me and Jeff followed up the rear so to speak. They followed me out of the office and to the lift. We went down to the car park level the vehicle was parked on and stepped out.

I pointed to the rental car and said, 'There it is there. The one covered in shit.'

John looked in disbelief at the state of the car as he marched towards it. I rushed around and opened all the doors and stepped back for him to do a proper inspection. I started to list the faults.

John stood there dumbfounded before said, 'What's that black shit all over the seats?'

'I think its engine oil and I think the white stuff is wool.'

'How the bloody hell would you get engine oil and wool into a police car for Christ's sake?'

He was speaking to no one in particular and was merely venting some of his building anger. After walking around the car he said, 'The whole bloody car's rooted. That wheel's bent, nearly every bloody panel is dented or scratched. The windscreen's cracked and the interior is not only looking like a tip, it's completely rooted. That shit will never come out.'

He turned to me and said, 'Did you ask the Boss what he did to it?'

'No I went straight to Jeff who went straight to you. I'm not going to say anything to him. He looks like he's still half pissed and he hates me anyway.'

John looked back at the car for several minutes and then ground his teeth through thinned lips and said, 'How the bloody hell am I going to cover this one? Lock it up and leave it there. I'll go and speak to him and see what the hell he's done with it.'

Everyone walked back to the lift and went back to the office, leaving John to find out what had happened. By pure chance, some half an hour later everyone was in the mess room having a tea and coffee, including John. He had already told me he had not been able to find the Boss. Not five minutes after we sat down in he marches. He looked a lot steadier on his feet but he still looked like a walking hangover. He strode in and stood there in an authoritarian pose with his big fat fists resting on his muffin top and said, 'So this is where everyone's hiding while I'm left to hold the fort.'

This was supposed to be funny, but as no one liked him, only a couple gave half-hearted pretend laughs to placate him. He made a coffee and sat down interrupting whoever was speaking at the time without excuse or apology.

He directed his question to John saying, 'So what's going on?'

John looked back at him and said, 'I have to speak to you about that car you brought back today. I'll talk to you in the office when we finish here.'

The Boss wasn't having any of that and said, 'Office. Bullshit. Just tell me here.'

John replied through gritted teeth, 'No it might be better in my office Boss.'

John was trying to save the stupid bastard from being embarrassed in front of the whole Task Force. Something he managed to do on numerous occasions without anybody's help.

'Will you just ask me whatever you're going to ask me. By the way that car's a heap of shit,' the Boss said.

He swung around and looked directly at me before asking in his usual ignorant tone, 'Did you tell that bloody dickhead at the rental joint that the boss said that car's a heap of shit?'

Initially I was surprised that he remembered it was me who he had given the keys and the instructions to. Before I had a chance to respond John said, 'What the hell did you do to that car? It's rooted.'

'What do you mean, what did I do to it. It's a heap of shit,' he replied.

'It's got a bent wheel and the tyre's half flat for a start and the bloody windscreen's cracked right across it,' John said.

'I hit a bloody big pothole and the bloody wheel bent. It's obviously cheap shit and they can get rooted. The windscreen was where a branch hit it and it cracked.'

'What's the bloody oil and wool in the back seat? It's covered in it,' John asked.

The Boss looked exasperated at being questioned and replied, 'If you've ever spent any time on a farm, you'd know you have to get shit moved around. I had to move an engine block from one side to the shed to get it fixed and it must've leaked a little bit of oil. I didn't take any notice of it to tell the truth.'

'You drove a bloody engine block around in a hire car?'

The Boss was starting to look a little uncomfortable when he said, 'What did you think I was going to do, push it around the bloody joint in a wheel barrow? And the wool is from two sheep that I had to bring back for crutching and to give them some of that scour shit. And listen here, I'm entitled to use the work car for private use anyway and that's what I did. So they can get rooted.'

'So what do we tell them when we take the car back? That's if we can drive the bloody thing in the first place. What about all the dents and scratches on the panels. Were they done on the farm too?' John asked.

'No smart arse, they weren't. I knocked the bloody pillar in the car park and the others are just normal wear and tear when you drive around a farm. Anyway, I've got work to do. You take the bloody thing back and make sure he gets told to give us decent cars from now on and not those shit Jap imports or whatever they are,' he said.

The Boss was in no way repentant and was more pissed off at having to explain himself in front of the troops. Something he could have avoided if he'd listened to John in the first place when he was given the chance. Not that there was anywhere lower to go in the estimates of the rest of the crew.

With that he finished his coffee and shoved his chair back and marched as best he could out of the mess room. John sat in his chair looking at everyone else and looked like he was about to pop a cork. 'That bloke's unbelievable,' he said. 'That's the third car he's rooted and he doesn't give a rat's arse.'

I was again tasked with taking the car back to the rental company, but this time I was accompanied by Jeff, who was not at all impressed. I drove the car with the bent wheel all the way to the rental company. Luckily, it was within five or six kilometres from the headquarters and I only had to endure the clunking of the bent wheel and the overwhelming stench inside the car for about 10 minutes. I drove with the window down all the way and had my head stuck out as often as I could.

I pulled up outside the small office and waited for the sergeant to pull in behind me and get out of the car.

Jeff looked at me and I laughed and said, 'Your move sergeant.'

This was a line from the sergeant's course where the blokes doing the course were presented with varying scenarios and then asked what they would do with 'Your move sergeant.'

Jeff looked back at me and smiled. 'Smart arse,' he said.

With that in he went and spoke to the poor young manager. He met him at the door, having seen us arrive in a heap of shit that unfortunately was his car. He stood just outside the door and was shown the inside by Jeff, ably assisted by me repeatedly interjecting, pointing out further faults that Jeff had not got around to yet. In the end the crest fallen manager just stood there and closed over his vehicle inspection folder. He stood there for what seemed ages just staring at the car then tears started rolling down his cheeks and dripped off his jaw onto his shirt. Neither Jeff nor I had anything to add.

Jeff patted the poor bugger on the shoulder and said, 'Mate, I'm so sorry. Whatever it costs to fix, just put it on our bill. This is a bloody disgrace and we're just the poor bastards who have to bring it back. If your boss needs to talk to me, just get him to give me a call.'

The young bloke did not respond as the tears kept welling and spilling down his face. That was how we left him as we drove off in the good car back to the office. Neither Jeff or I made any funny, smart arse or derogatory comments about the manager. In fact, we both felt terrible for the poor bugger. As if his predicament was not bad enough. He told Jeff the Police Department were months behind in their payments as it was and now he has to report this to his boss.

We returned to the office and updated John who was as mad as a cut snake over the complete and utter disregard with which the boss showed to his job and his tools of trade. It did nothing either for the troops than reinforce what an incompetent, useless, ignorant bastard some people were and we all hoped that one day he would be held accountable for his actions. He never was.

CHAPTER TWENTY THREE

Witness Protection

On Thursday 13 July 1989 we started looking after a filthy mole we will refer to as Witness X, wife of a career criminal, lover of another career criminal who even worked with her hubby at times and someone a couple of coppers couldn't resist the charms of.

She allegedly managed to sleep with at least one and possibly more of the protection teams that would look after her for over a year leading up to the Walsh Street court case.

She was the very public face and de facto of one of the key figures in the Walsh Street Investigation. She entered the Witness Protection Scheme and played most of her captors on a break. Some will argue otherwise but to the proof is in the pudding.

She was lucky she got to enter anything that day, as she came very close to joining some of her friends who had departed this earth early by some involvement of drugs, guns, violence or a cocktail of some or all of the above. She had been in close contact with one of the investigating detectives we will call Detective X and was going to come under his wing that day. However, they'd been spotted at a Port Melbourne coffee shop at one of their 'secret meetings' leading up to her coming over to the light side. It was at one of these meetings that Detective X showed her letters from her dear husband to another woman he had been sleeping with unbeknownst to her. For a bloke who at this stage had apparently infiltrated some Mafia drug network in his police service, I cannot understand why he would meet someone in a public venue like he did. This was a very high risk move and one that that almost backfired with tragic consequences. Anyway, they did and she got spotted by someone who knew her and they in turn let the crooks and their legal representatives know. Good start. Not.

After that meeting Detective X kept in touch with her by phone and they picked a day and had arrangements as close to tied down as anyone could when dealing with people like her. He spoke to her about lunch time that day and she had visitors. By the end of that day, after finally getting back in touch with her, he could tell that she was zonked off her tits on drugs and alcohol and he called one of the bosses who organised the local CIB to execute a Drug Warrant on her premises. This took time and she'd been given heroin at least twice that day by one of her husband's friends and she normally didn't use heroin. The concern then became that friends of his were obviously concerned about her and perhaps thought the best way to keep her quiet was to kill her. If the dose or strength of the heroin was too much, death is the result and the process is referred to as giving someone a 'hot shot'. This was common practice for these notorious drug families as a means of protecting their interests, or in exacting revenge on anyone they suspected of becoming a 'dog' or police informer.

I remember when we collected Witness X and escorted her back to St Kilda Road for her first night in protection. She was more than a little under the weather and was suitably slurred in her speech and her eyes told the story. The fact she had been injected with heroin by someone else had put the fear of our Lord into her and she knew if she hadn't been rescued that day she had most likely ended up on a slab at the morgue. Looking back that might not have been such a tragedy. But some of these scumbags are harder to kill than cockroaches.

When we got her out of the car in the underground car park, we walked her up the concrete stairwells that led to the foyer where the lift was then accessible to the upper floors. I had a healthy disregard for her and was finding it difficult to look at her with as purely protective objective as I should have. As she walked up the stairs in front of me, I decided to chamber a round from the shotgun I was carrying, just to make sure I was ready to roll should anything untoward happen.

I unloaded the shotgun when I placed it in the boot of the unmarked police car, as was the procedure for safe storage and transporting firearms, especially a shotgun. After I had loaded the 5 into the magazine, I decided to load one up the spout and rather than insert it directly, I thought I might see what her reflexes were like and pump a round into the chamber. She had walked past me and must have picked up on the negative vibes I was giving off and she looked at me with a look of distrust and hatred. I smiled at her and as she passed me and went up the stairs she had a couple of sneaky peeps at me over her shoulder. I think the fact that I was standing there with the shotgun made her uncomfortable for some reason. As we proceeded up the stairs, I chambered the round and the shotgun made the noise they make when this happens. As I did this, I had the shotgun pointed at the stairs at the back of her. When she heard me rack the shotty, she spun her head around like Linda Blair and looked at me with absolute terror in her eyes and her knees went week. I saw her distress and said something soothing to calm her. Not. From then on she called me Cowboy and often told the story of how she thought I was going to 'knock' her in the stairwell that night. I must say it still brings a smile to my face today thinking of our misunderstanding.

By the time she came into witness protection, there had been a complete breakdown in communications and the Task Force was split in two. Officer X had Detective X, together known as The Dynamic Duo, ably assisting him and his undercover prowess in criminal investigation techniques came to the fore.

As soon as she came into protection, her first request was that she didn't want to deal with John Noonan, Jim O'Brien or Col Ryan. She had allegedly made this request to The Dynamic Duo, who then dutifully informed the brass of her wish. A more suspicious person than me would probably think that her request may have been assisted by her new 'controllers'. Unfortunately, in the wash up, who was actually controlling who became more evident.

The orders came down from the chiefs that these three be kept away from her and should not be furnished copies or summaries of what she said to The Dynamic Duo. I am of the opinion that the hierarchy were so glad that they'd got Witness X to 'flip' on her husband and family that they would have given in to any of her requests. And the fact that the request disadvantaged John Noonan only made the orders sweeter.

They had Task Force detectives performing the protection detail to maintain uniformity of personnel and to make sure that if she came out with anything at any stage that was relative to the job it would not be missed.

When she was taken into protection she had been switched from motels close by the task force centre of operations. This was due to the fact that she was being interviewed and making statements almost daily and the other detectives doing the statements wanted her close by should they need anything.

To add insult to injury it was decided the remaining six detectives John Noonan had left on his team, including me, had to provide 24-hour protection on the new star witness. This left him alone in preparing the already overdue Brief of Evidence against the three charged with the murders of Steve Tynan and Damien Eyre. There were numerous court appearances where the defendant's legal representatives criticised the continual delays in bringing the murder charges to court. Little did they know the whole thing was being done by one bloke at this stage in John Noonan.

As I had already had the stand-up blue with Officer X in the Homicide offices a short time prior to Witness X entering protection, I thought my days on the Task Force would be numbered. Miraculously I was left in and was granted the dubious honour of being on the witness protection detail to look after her for the next four weeks or so. I was ably accompanied by Geoff Calderbank, Billy Panagiotaros, Fiona Richardson, Constable Andrea Wassall and we always had a Special Operations Group member with us with the heavy firepower in the form of a machine pistol which was keep in a silver hard cover briefcase, similar to a camera case.

Witness X was a woman in her early thirties and was the typical crook's missus. She had dyed blonde hair, a skinny build with pock marked skin, and looked closer to the start of Darwin's evolution line than the finish. She had two sons, one was nine or 10 years of age and the other about six years. She also had a three-year-old daughter who was a cute little kid, or so it seemed to the unwary. She was rough as an uncut pineapple and was cunning as a shit house rat and never stopped trying to 'play' the protection details that were looking after her.

At this stage of the operation she was being kept in a very nice modern three-bedroom apartment in South Yarra, the very nice inner-city suburb of Melbourne It was well secluded with a high hedge at the front that blocked the view from the busy Punt Road and pedestrian traffic was none the wiser what or who was on the other side. My detail had been looking after her at this location for a couple of days and at that stage she wasn't required at the operations centre. So we were stuck with her and had to stay close and remain on high alert.

She was a foul-mouthed sex maniac who did her best to bed whoever was looking after her, regardless of the sex of the coppers. She had a matching sense of humour that made me blush or sick in the stomach, depending on the topic under discussion.

I remember the first week of looking after Witness X in a magnificent apartment at The Como Hotel. She had been transported back to the motel after making statements all day. She returned to the safe house in a foul mood and was going off tap about anything and everything. A couple of minutes later, after she had gone to the bedroom to see the daughter, I heard a piercing scream. As we all bounded towards the room, we could hear the thud of punches being landed on bare skin. I burst into the bedroom to see her kneeling on her daughter's stomach, while punching her with a closed fist to the face and head. I rushed at the bed and grabbed her long hair and wrenched her off the little one. 'What do you think you're doing?' I said.

She spat back, 'That fucking little slut ate my chocolate and then gave me a fuckin' mouthful of cheek. So I was beltin some of the shit out of her.'

I looked over my shoulder and saw Andrea Wassall tending to little one on the bed where she lay semi-conscious and bleeding from the nose, one eye and her mouth. She already had a fat lip and both eyes were starting to swell shut and go a bluish colour.

I was mad as a cut snake and turned back to Witness X, who I was holding in a vice like grip, while pushing her back and up a glass mirror sliding door to restrain her.

I spoke through clenched teeth to her and said, 'You listen to me. If I ever catch you laying a finger on that kid, don't worry about anyone else trying to kill you. I'll put a bullet through that ugly fucking head of yours myself. Do you understand me?'

There ensued a brief but spirited discussion of her thoughts on us and our thoughts of her. The last bit I yelled through clenched teeth and sprayed spittle all over her face which made her blink to try and avoid it. She held out for a few more seconds and then nodded her head as much as she could in agreement.

By this stage, the little one was starting to come good and took in what was happening around her. She never shed a tear and lay there looking at me with her mother. She raised herself to a sitting position and with hatred burning brightly in her little eyes she yelled as best she could at me saying, 'Get off me fuckin' mum. You fuckin' dog.' Charming.

The manner Witness X was kept in witness protection was unbelievable for all of us looking after her. The day we took her there some clever dick Detective X was supposed to organise the booking as the B Team were not to have anything to do with her, other than keep her alive. With his apparent vast knowledge of being undercover himself, he would be the best to organise the accommodation, keeping in mind the delicacy required in maintaining our cover story. The idea was to be able to walk in, check in and get the witness to the secure room as soon as possible and do our best to ensure she was not seen by anyone.

We strolled into the foyer of this very upmarket motel called The Como, leaving Witness X being guarded by one of the soggies, Bill Panagiotaros and Andrea Wassall. We spoke to the clerk at the reception desk and told him we had a booking made by Detective X. The clerk checks and cannot find any such booking. We tried all of our surnames with no success. We cannot ask if there is a

booking for Victoria Police for a witness in protection so we have
to stand there looking like dickheads. We make up some lame story
and tell the bloke we will double check and get back to him. We
went back to the car to use the radio to check with the detective.
The sergeant Geoff Calderbank returns about 10 minutes later
looking flushed in the face and not very happy with the world.

I approached him and said, 'What's the go?'

'Do you know what name that dickhead booked us under?'
he replied.

'No. What?'

'He booked under the name Condor.'

'Why would he book it in Condor? How are we going to give
any identification in the name of Condor?'

He shakes his head and replies through gritted teeth, 'He
remembered it from a spy movie or some shit and thought it'd
be cool if he made the booking in that name. He's a dickhead.
Fair dinkum.'

We then had to make the booking in one of our names.

Calderbank was furious and we never let Detective X forget
what a moron he was for his Condor booking. This was to be one
of a number of unbelievably stupid actions and requests during that
four-week period that showed how incompetence and gullibility
can be used to devastating effect.

While she was still at The Como in her luxury suite, Detective
X managed to have some down time and had what I think was his
30th birthday party in her witness protection apartment. Apparently
he wanted to do something special to commemorate the occasion.
Unbelievably he must have spoken to his witness in protection
about it, because she apparently suggested he have his birthday
party at 'her' apartment.

What was more surprising was that apparently the police department had paid for his soirée. All the accounts to do with the witness protection were handled and approved for payment by one of the bosses.

The separation of work from play became even more blurred than it already was. Normally a witness was kept in third rate motels or rented properties and we never provided half of the luxuries and treats she was provided. There should always be a distance kept between the witness and the handlers to maintain the integrity of the association, not to mention to prevent any accusation or implication at court proceedings that the witness was only saying what she was told to maintain her position with the investigators. Anything out of the usual benefits would be used to accuse the investigators of providing inducements to obtain the evidence they obtained. If the defence had have known some of these incidents had taken place prior to the court proceedings, there would have been hell to pay.

As it was, she never gave evidence and flipped on The Dynamic Duo, effectively scuttling the prosecution case. The management of Witness X during that four to six weeks was, apart from being unconventional, bordering on the ridiculous.

CHAPTER TWENTY FOUR

The Witness Needs Romance

We were called into a meeting at the Task Force office where we were met by The Dynamic Duo who were still 'managing' the witness protection for Witness X. I think it was Officer X who said 'Listen we are having some problems with Witness X. She's not very happy at the moment and reckons she needs a root.'

He continued saying, 'No listen I'm serious. We need to take her out somewhere up the bush or something and let her have a few drinks and try and get her a root.'

We looked at each other and said, 'You've got to be joking aren't you? I'm not taking that dirty mole out to get her a root'.

He responded with, 'No listen, we've talked about it and it was actually our idea and I reckon it'll do wonders to give her a bit of tension relief and get her happy again. We've still got a shitload of statements to get off her about various jobs her hubbie's gang did, so we have to keep her happy. We think the best place to take her is to a country town big enough to have a disco or nightclub where she might find someone of her social standing. I was thinking Ballarat.' He smiled and sat there looking at us.

'Hey, if you like the mole so much, why don't you take her to Ballarat and get her a root?' I said.

They must have sensed my dislike for one of them in particular, that being Detective X, and he immediately responded and said,

'No. We've got a stack to do from the statements we've taken and it'll give us a great opportunity to catch up and check out what she's told us already. So I'll get you blokes and one soggie. Oh and you better take Andrea with you because it'd be good to have a female with her to keep an eye on her.'

One of our blokes said, 'And how are we going to look with the mole, with the lovely Andrea, the three of us and the bloody soggie. We're going to stick out like dog's balls in any nightclub anywhere, let alone in the bush.'

'I want you to take her up on Friday night and let her pick up someone, root him and then piss him off and come back with her happy,' Officer X said.

'Just tell anyone who asks that she's your cousin from interstate or something and that you haven't seen her in years. No one'll think anything,' Detective X added.

So the arrangements were made to leave Melbourne on the Friday afternoon and head to Ballarat in a two car convoy. Billy Panagiotaros drove the lead car with Geoff Calderbank and I drove the trail car with Witness X, Andrea and the Soggie. We drove all the way to Ballarat and checked into a motel, right behind a pub that had a disco, which was directly in front of the motel.

As the police department was more than generous with their allowances, we were allowed to book two rooms. We were all in plain civilian clothes and she was dressed like she normally was, in tight faded blue jeans and an off-white shirt that looked too small for her but she thought was great because it made her tits look bigger. At about 8pm we head over to the disco and were about the only ones in there to begin with. Geoff Calderbank and I sat at one table with Billy Panagiotaros and the Soggie. Andrea Wassall had to sit drinking with Witness X, trying to make it look like two girls on a night out. We all had a beer and were checking out our less than salubrious surroundings, moaning what a shit job this was. The Soggie was a good bloke and he had to sit with his silver briefcase that held the machine pistol. He had a few drinks and we sat there watching everyone who arrived giving them a cursory once over.

Before an hour was up the place was about three quarters full of some of the scummiest excuses for human beings I had seen assembled outside some B grade zombie movie. Most of the blokes were decked out in a blue singlet, or better known as a wife beater, with jeans, boots and long, dirty looking hair. One bloke who looked pretty pissed approached the girl's table and ended up sitting down and talking with his eye firmly on the prize, Witness X. She was lit up like a Christmas tree at the interest being shown to her by this Neanderthal. He had over shoulder length hair and had his two front teeth missing. He had some of his dinner on the front of his wife beater and homemade tatts all over his arms and hands. I went over and sat next to Andrea and pretended to chat her up, which I was actually trying to do, as she was very tidy looking and was a great girl. I was introduced to Romeo and quickly worked out he was dumb as dog shit and smelled appropriately. Andrea was complaining that he stank and was a low life. I laughed and was whispering to her to try and enjoy her cousin's company and if she was lucky, she could take me home.

The first spark of romance was lit when Witness X leaned over and kissed Romeo. She was as drunk as he was by this time and their passionate kiss looked like she was stoned and trying to suck an icy pole. It was one of the most grotesque sights I had seen. Even from our new vantage point, which was a couple of tables away, I could see the fervour with which she bent to her task. Romeo thought he had died and gone to heaven.

On my next visit to the table on the pretext of talking to Andrea, Romeo could not contain himself. He said, 'Hey mate. How fucking good's this. She's a fucking horn bag.'

In those days describing someone of the opposite sex as a 'horn bag' was actually the highest compliment a single male could bestow. I did my best to suppress my desire to lean over and assist with the violent extraction of a couple more of his less than pearly white teeth. I agreed and tried to be civil in a fashion that would be acknowledged by Romeo.

At one stage a mate of Romeo's appeared and was trying to chat up Andrea. She was polite but aloof without being standoffish. This bloke told Andrea straight up he had a girlfriend and would not be playing up. He then produced his wallet from his jeans and showed her a picture of his missus. It was a motorbike. Yep that's right a motorbike. That relationship did not grow at all and Andrea ended up telling her suitor it was time to hop on his girlfriend and fuck off. In the nicest possible way of course.

It was after midnight when the disco was packing up and Witness X was now firmly entrenched with her new beau. The sarge spoke to her and went over the instructions again. He told her to take him to the room on the left. Get the business done and when we knock on the door he has to go. She was pissed as a parrot at this stage and was happy as a pig in poo. She spoke to Romeo and he got off his stool as fast as he could in his drunken state. They walked out and the rest of us followed.

Romeo kept looking at us with distrust at our level of interest into her welfare. As we crossed the car park towards the rooms he said, 'What is the go with your mates?'

'They're me cousins. Aaah Haaa,' she replied.

The sarge opened the door to the room and they staggered in hand in hand with her laughing.

'Now don't be all night. We only have two rooms,' he said.

'You can watch if you want Cuz,' she said.

She laughed out loud at his glare which needed no response. He walked back into the room next door where we were all lounging on the bed or sitting in the pair of chairs. He looked at all of us when he walked in and did not need to say anything. He just shook his head and sat on the end of the double bed.

I was reclining on the single bed which was up against the front window of the room, with the double bed on my left towards the middle of the room and then another single bed on the far end.

They were left alone for over an hour and then with no noise coming from next door the sarge said, 'That's long enough.' He rose from his perch on the end of the double bed and was joined by the Soggie and me. We walked outside our room and checked with Billy, who had been keeping watch outside the room to make sure she didn't get any ideas of eloping with her new love. The sarge knocked on the door and said, 'Righto. Time's up. Tell your boyfriend he has to go home.'

'Oh fuck off will ya. We only done it once,' she said.

She was then joined by Romeo who yelled, 'Fuck off will youse.'

Romeo could not pronounce the f in the word fuck as he had two missing front teeth. The air escaped through the gap instead of reverberating off his teeth to allow the formation of the word. It consequently turned the word into uck and transformed th into a v. As in 'vis is not good', instead of this is not good.

We put the key in the lock and opened the door to their room. Witness X lay on the bed and pretended to be shocked at our unwelcome intrusion. The sarge stood at the end of the bed and said to Romeo, 'OK mate, grab your gear and head off.'

Romeo lay back naked on top of the bed sheet with his head resting on his tattooed forearm. He was peering with half opened eyes, due in part to him being pissed and the other part being he was trying to appear tough. He lunged as best he could off the bed and made an aggressive move towards us. He didn't get two feet when three pistols were levelled at his head. He stopped dead in his tracks and was grabbed by the Soggie who suggested he get dressed and leave. His bravado had evaporated and he fumbled with his clothing whilst trying to dress himself. He kept raising his hands in mock surrender and saying, 'Alright. Alright. Don't shoot me for fuck's sake.'

Each time he fumbled or looked directly at his predicament, he would lose the grip on either his jeans, which he was still trying to do up, or he was dropping his other possessions in a scrambled attempt to depart post haste. He managed to get his jeans on and had his arms full of his singlet, socks and smokes. He was assisted out of the room and ushered into the car park bare footed and still had the front of his jeans undone with his belt hanging from the gaping front of his jeans.

'What the fuck is goin on here? Your cousins are fuckin crazy,' he said.

As he walked past me I caught a whiff of his unique mix of alcohol, cigarettes, perspiration and fresh sex. He was pushed out by the Soggie and before he had made it five steps into the car park, he was accidentally hit in the back of his head by one of his work boots and in the middle of the back with the other. Someone had thrown them with more than required gusto and said, 'Now piss off back to the piggery or wherever you crawled out of.' He was going to reply again but instead gathered up his gear and beat a hasty retreat away from the three of us. Once we were sure he had gone we went back into the room.

'Righto get dressed and get out of the bed. The fun's over for the night,' the Sarge said.

Witness X was still half cut and laughing while holding the bed sheet over her naked frame. We all walked out the front and I lit up a smoke and looked at the sarge.

'How bad is this? This is bullshit. Are we coppers or bloody pimps?' I said.

He shook his head and looked at his feet before saying, 'Well I can definitely say it is the first time in my police career that I've had to do this. That's for sure.'

Witness X appeared in the doorway of the room and leaned on the frame with one arm extended over her head in an attempt at a provocative pose and said, 'Whose next boys?'

We all leered at her and one of us said, 'In your dreams.'

We were up early the next morning and made arrangements to move out and head back to Melbourne. I drove the car with the sarge and the others stayed chaperone for Witness X in the second car. The drive back was quiet and I could see that everyone was still hyper vigilant and angry at what we had just been through. Apparently, the other car was just as quiet, as she slept most of the way back, due to the dual effects of the grog and the physical exertion. We were never so happy to get her back to the safe house and organise the changeover of the protection crews.

So witness protection isn't such a bad gig if you happen to crack on to a couple of new age guys like the Dynamic Duo. I still get hot under the collar that we were asked to do what we were. I wish we would have said no and suffered the consequences.

Witness X stayed in our protective custody until 14 August 1989. She then went into the mainstream WITSEC program which was run by the Protective Security Group or PSG. The change from luxury apartments and being fawned upon by doting 'controllers' to standard rental properties and ordinary motels where she was protected by rank and file coppers didn't sit well with her. Her ability to influence and control were quite amazing and she managed to run the protection crews ragged.

Allegations that she got on a little too closely with several of the protection team members seemed to have been confirmed recently if that was required. A television special on Walsh Street contained a section where they interviewed one of the coppers who had looked after her. The accusation was that the lines between controllers and the controlled had been blurred beyond recognition and that over fraternisation with her minders was regularly mentioned. This bloke they interviewed then made a comment that when I heard it, I nearly fell out of my chair. The gist of what he said was that it was only natural when police look after a witness for so long that they would become close.

Maybe his idea of 'becoming close' and mine are somewhat different. The very thought that a copper would become intimate with Witness X, no matter what the circumstances, are unbelievable. She was the epitome of disgusting to me, not only in her looks but her behaviour and other qualities. She had become the controller and manipulated her way around witness protection policy and procedures and had the coppers dancing to her tune. She did everything from try and commit suicide, shoplift, try her best to bed as many as possible and even managed to call her hubby in prison from one of her supposed safe houses. She stayed on board for her evidence to be used at the committal proceedings, which got the three charged at that stage committed for trial. The fourth was directly presented for trial after the committal. Whether she ever had any intention of giving evidence at the trial no one except her will ever know. Either way, the delay between her entering protection and the case getting up in court was far too long and made the task of keeping protected witnesses happy, extremely difficult.

CHAPTER TWENTY FIVE

Life After Walsh Street

After the witness protection was concluded on Witness X, we were told that we would be returning to our squads and for me that was the Major Crime Squad. We were 'allowed' to wrap up whatever we had been working on and believe me, the investigation was not over at that stage. It was effectively being cut short and detectives who had worked their arses off were sent packing without even a thankyou from Force Command or anyone else supposedly in charge of our task force.

I got back to the Major Crime Office after taking a few days off and part of me thought I was happy to be out of a most toxic of environments that was the Task Force. I think all of us carried a great deal of resentment and felt somewhat ostracised from the rest of the force for whatever reason, real or imagined.

At the start of that job we were proud to be on it and put in more than anyone could reasonably have expected. At the end I know I was full of anger, distrust and contempt for the police force and its unprofessional treatment of us. I thought my time of being harassed by some of the brass was over. Silly me.

On whatever the day was that I returned to the Major Crime Squad, I walked in and got reacquainted with the boys and by this stage Col Florence and Peter Spence were both Senior Sergeants.

After I had said my hello to everyone I was called into an office with Peter Spence. He told me I had to report to the boss, a Detective Inspector. I asked him why and he said he did not know but that the boss wanted to see me before I settled in. I started racking my brain for what the cause of the summons could be. Due to what had gone on at the Task Force I already had a decent slice of paranoia and once again it was to prove accurate. I walked around to the boss' office and he told me to take a seat. He looked like I had just asked his daughter out on a date and was not very happy whatever the reason. I sat down and asked what was going on. He told me I was being returned to the Bull Pen at Russell Street. The Bull Pen was where you went if you were brand new to the CIB or had got into trouble for whatever reason and had to do penance. I asked again what the hell was going on and started to get angry at what I was being told. He told me I had been accused of assaulting an officer and that I was being sent to Russell Street as a result of this most serious offence.

I could not believe it. I had just worked on the biggest job I had ever been on and done my best. I was owed in the vicinity of 20 weeks leave and days off that were held over in lieu from the Task Force. We very rarely had days off and we definitely did not take leave. In fact, I had to sit for my sergeant's exams on my own, as I missed them due to not being able to study whilst at the Task Force. With a week's study under my belt I sat and passed all my exams and was then eligible to do my sergeants board and try and get onto the sergeant's course. I had proven yet again that cream rises to the top. What a champion.

I asked who I was alleged to have assaulted. He sat back in his chair and told me there was one officer, one senior detective and a civilian. I could not believe what I was hearing. I asked who they were and what I was supposed to have done. He elaborated and told me the officer I was supposed to have assaulted was none other than Officer X. I nearly laughed, although I in no way found it funny. I knew that someone in the hierarchy was obviously trying to finish me off and make sure my police career was over. I felt a rush of blood and if he would have been there, I would have belted him and been quite happy to nod the head to it. I asked where I was alleged to have assaulted him. He told me it had occurred in an interview room in the Homicide Squad office some months ago. I instantly remembered the day I had gone off at him in the interview room and I relayed exactly what had happened. I told him this was absolute bullshit and that Officer X was a lying bastard. I asked who the other detective was. He looked at me and genuinely seemed surprised. He said in fact it was the bloke I had jokingly suggested, Detective X. I was furious. I could not stand the prick, but I had never laid a glove on the weak bastard. He told me I had allegedly waited for this detective in the car park at the Old Police Club in Mackenzie Street behind the old Russell Street Police Complex and 'King Hit' him from behind as he walked out.

I reckon I was bordering somewhere between shock and some form of malevolence I had never felt before. I told the boss I definitely could not stand the bloke as he was a weak gutted lying bastard as well. I told him how we were at the Police Club one night and I was talking to some blokes from the Majors while enjoying a beer or twenty. Whoever I was talking to, I was bagging Detective X in no uncertain terms and was telling my drinking buddies not to trust him, no matter how good a bloke they thought he was. As I was doing so, up he walks and stands glaring at me and he asked what I was saying. I told him exactly what I was saying and told him to his face I thought he was a two faced, gutless prick who should have been sacked over some of the shit he had done. He pursed his lips as he was want to do and I didn't know whether to take that as a sign he intended to kiss me or he was pretending to be a nasty little bitch.

We exchanged words and then he did what I never thought he would do. He asked me outside. I could not believe it. I finished my beer in one gulp and put it back on the bar and turned to him and said, 'Righto let's go'.

He went red in the face and stood there looking at me and said, 'Hang on I've just got a drink.'

I said, 'What do you mean. What do I have to do? Make an appointment? You just asked me outside so put your drink down and come out now.'

So that was how it started and out we went. A few blokes followed us out and a couple of blokes who were both at the SOG at that stage, who happened to be in the bar, also came out. I had to do a double take when they intervened and tried to talk us out of it. The SOG were trying to stop people from fighting. They were noted for being absolute maniacs on the grog and would regularly end up fighting each other or anyone else within arm's reach. I knew they could all fight like thrashing machines and I think a healthy dose of competition within the group worked wonders for having the typical Alpha Male pissing competition which was normally over something stupid.

So there I was being counselled by these blokes. I knew both of them having worked with them on a couple of jobs with the Major Crime and the task force. After a couple of minutes of earnest discussion, a couple of drunken blokes walked past our group in the car park and yelled something at one of the soggies. That was it. The conciliation was abruptly suspended and the next thing the soggie is about to unleash on these two unsuspecting big mouths, who were of a good size and were both bigger than him. Somehow that battle was averted, I think mainly because they had seen the crazy look in his eyes as he stood there ready to rumble.

After that was over back we went to the car park where we had been and took up our pre interruption positions. I looked at Detective X and said, 'Come on. Stop mucking around. You asked me out so you can throw the first punch.'

He stood there like he was in a trance and then he burst out crying. I stood there and was even feeling bad for this gutless bastard. I wasn't all that well versed with the rules of engagement but somehow I didn't think sooking up was part of it.

'You're shitting me aren't you. You ask me out and then you start crying. You gutless prick,' I said.

He was almost collapsing in on himself and was actually sobbing. He was comforted by one of the bystanders and I went back into the club and continued drinking. I don't know what happened to him, but I don't remember him coming back into the club after his breakdown. I left with another couple of the Majors and we went on somewhere else from there. I did not hit him and I most certainly did not ambush and King Hit him with his back to me.

I finished up by asking the boss if he wanted me to call these blokes and let them tell him themselves what had happened that night. Then I asked who the other one I was supposed to have hit was. He told me it was none other than a very well-known police reporter from one of the major dailies in Melbourne. I am sure this was over words I had with him at an Irish pub in Melbourne where the Homicide Squad had one of their functions. I do not recall exactly what it was over, but I know it was something to do with my brother and I had taken umbrage to it. We did not come to blows and he left the function and that was that. That was only real interaction I had with him and so it had to be that instance I was being accused of hitting him. No doubt one of the Homicide Squad had seen this and must have made mention of it to someone, in its revised format, to come back and try and do me for it.

I think from there we had to go and see the detective superintendent and I was most graciously allowed to resume my position at the Majors, without having to suffer the ignominy of being sent back to the Bull Pen.

All this left me with a very bitter taste in my mouth. I could not believe how hard and how far these blokes in the upper echelons of the police force would go to get at someone. I could now see what was going on more clearly and I knew it would not stop. I could either shut up or put up with their continued harassment for the rest of what was going to be my career and lose a little bit of what it was that made me who I was.

I could not stand bullies, thugs or people who thought they were better than me. This is where I first came across the saying 'It is better to die on your feet than live on your knees'.

I decided to resign and do something else with my life.

I must say it wasn't the ending I thought my police service would have and it was sad it came to the end it did. I loved being a copper up until Walsh Street and had proven myself to be a more than capable policeman and detective. I had let the police force dictate my life and had never said no. I had done more than anyone should reasonably be expected to do for their employer. But that is what it was like.

The job was your life. Everything else became secondary and I know that is why so many married police end up separated or divorced. There were plenty on the task force that had their marriages and relationships irreparably damaged due to the call of duty. The hours away from family and spouses were more than should ever have been allowed.

That was the way it was in those days. You had to do things you might not want to and when you might not want to do them. The only good thing for me was I met my wife of over 20 years, Andrea

Noonan, on that Task Force and we had three beautiful children together. Unfortunately, my marriage has had to endure more stresses that it should have and that has not bode well for us.

I left the force and went and did some other adventures in Australia and beyond over the next twenty years up until I wrote this book. I have done everything I wanted to do and don't have any regrets. At least I will not die wondering.

CHAPTER TWENTY SIX

Fast Forward to Today

It is fast approaching 30 years since I left the police force. Initially it was a difficult transition and I missed the blokes more than the job. The nasty taste in my mouth from the task force would not be refreshed. The political bastardry and leadership ineptitude had combined to dissolve the once strong bond between myself and the force.

I have over that period worked around Australia and spent three years in Papua New Guinea. I have experienced great successes and great failures. I made a lot and I managed to lose a lot. But the experience of life is something money cannot change.

When there are two people on my porch in my later years, hopefully my beautiful fiancé Susan and myself, I will be satisfied I had a go at numerous adventures and made it to old age. I have outlived some very good friends and nearly the whole remaining cast from the crook's side of the Walsh Street Task Force. Victor Peirce and Anthony Farrell have joined their mates Jedd Houghton and Gary Abdullah in the not too flash area of the afterlife.

Surprisingly, none of these crew repented on their evil ways and became priests, doctors or educators. They stayed in their trade of drugs and violence that ultimately took everything from them.

VICTOR PEIRCE

Victor George Peirce was shot dead in Port Melbourne on Wednesday 1 May 2002. He had apparently turned a new leaf after getting out of jail around 2008 and became the perfect husband. The police alleged he was running a pill press selling ecstasy while working by day as a crane driver at the docks in Port Melbourne. Who knows and who really cares?

Some say it was a rip off over a drug deal where Victor was to be collecting cash but collected lead instead. He was shot several times by Andrew 'Benji' Veniamin in Bay Street Port Melbourne. The driver for Benji was found to have been Faruk Orman who was sentenced to 14 years jail in November 2009, although he was referred to as an unnamed man until his name was finally released in 2013.

Benji Veniamin was part of the Carlton Crew and was the right-hand man for his now deceased bestie Carl Williams. He is alleged to have killed or had some part in the deaths of numerous 'underworld' figures including Dino Dibra, Paul Kallipolitis, Graham 'The Munster' Kinniburgh and of course Victor Peirce among others.

Again, the life of living by the sword has the much-vaunted death by the same means. He was shot dead by Mick Gatto in a restaurant in Carlton in March 2004. It was alleged and accepted at trial that he pulled a 38 calibre pistol on Gatto who after a struggle popped one through the neck and another through one eye of Veniamin. Not unsurprisingly this had an adverse effect on poor old Benji's short and long-term medical conditions. He obviously wasn't made of the same stuff as one of the ladies of crime who got shot in the eye in her younger years and lived a long life.

WITNESS X

Witness X would have been distraught after losing the love of her life. Some men in her in life must have been full of magnets, perishing after attracting too much lead.

Her fall from grace over the decades has seen her publicly restate the evidence she was going to give at the Walsh Street trial that Criminal X had planned and taken an active role as one of the shooters at the Walsh Street murders. Her life has turned full circle and she apparently lives in a housing commission flat and is on welfare payments.

I remember her relating a story to us of Dennis Allen shooting one of his best mates who was like a brother to him. The thought was that this bloke was a 'dog', which was their language for a police informer. Dennis was at the peak of his powers at that stage revelling in the notoriety of being one of if not the biggest drug dealing syndicate in the country.

She told us he shot this hapless 'brother' in the shoulder. He then walked over to where he was sitting grimacing in pain and asked the brother if he thought he was going to kill him. The nervous and pain ridden brother laughs and says he did, obviously hoping that was the case and that he was just another innocent victim of the deranged drug addict Dennis.

According to Witness X, Dennis laughs with him holding his shoulders whilst standing behind him. He then raises the pistol and shoots him in the head, killing him. Apparently, she was in the kitchen having a cool can of beer with another of the female clan members. Criminal X and one of the other brothers were in the lounge when the shooting happened in front of them. They were shocked at the sudden demise of their other brother.

Allegedly Dennis then instructs Victor to put the dead brother into a 44-gallon drum and dump him in the Yarra River before heading to the pub for a cooly. They dutifully get the 44-gallon drum and tip the dead brother headfirst into it in the loungeroom. Naturally, the legs are sticking out and will not fit in. The decision is made they will have to cut the legs off with a chainsaw.

Criminal X gets the chainsaw, cranks it up and begins the gruesome task of severing the legs in the lounge room. Not suited for this task he throws up and can't continue. Allegedly, the other female present skulls her can and stands up and goes to inspect the proceedings. She allegedly calls her darling relative Criminal X a weak cunt and says, 'Here give it to me'. Wearing an apron to protect her tracksuit or similar stylish attire of those times, she proceeds to cut the legs off the dead bloke in the lounge room. It was good she was possessed of such project management skills that she thought about the consequences and took precautions not to have bits of leg all over everything.

Witness X said she came back into the kitchen covered in blood and bone and takes off the apron and washes up in the kitchen sink. As you would. She then gets a fresh can out of the fridge and cracks it open, commenting as she did what a weak prick Witness X's dear husband is. She then sits down and continues her conversation where it was left before her call to duty.

Baby X, as she was referred to during her mother's interactions with the TyeEyre Task Force, died of what was a suspected heroin overdose in December 2009. She was thought to have had a bad heroin addiction, no doubt brought on by her upbringing and life of crime thereafter.

In a peculiar twist, my ex-wife, who I met on the task force and later married, left the police force around the same time as me in about 1990. We had three children before she decided to re-join the police force around 2008. She had been part of the protection team during the task force and this was where we met. When she went back to the police force, her first posting was to Rowville and one of the first jobs she went to there was a bigger Baby X. It was thought she had a raging heroin addiction at that time.

Baby X really had no chance in life and what a hit for the karma train for Witness X and her dear hubby. Their darling daughter was the victim of the vile trade in illicit drugs they had profited so handsomely from for decades. They had built their families ill-gotten gains on trading in the misery of others. Now their own flesh and blood was reduced to the life of the walking dead, stealing and doing whatever she must to pay the piper. I hope all involved with the predelinquent perversion of this child are kept awake at night picturing her torture as thousands of other parents must have because of their trade in misery.

So that happy family have certainly fallen on hard times. Dad dead. Mum broke and living in housing commission. Their only daughter dead. I don't know what became of the other kids. They must still be with us in some shape or form or they too would have their own paragraph on Wikipedia like their beloved little sister and dad.

ANTHONY LEIGH FARRELL

One of the four men charged with the murders of Constables Tynan and Eyre was Anthony Leigh Farrell. He was acquitted of the murders but his life went from acquittal to a life of abuse and petty crime. He was never thought to have been at the scene of the shootings but was believed to have taken part in the planning. He died from cancer on 3 November 2018 at the age of 52. There's not much to say about this bloke. The world is a better place without him.

TREVOR PETTINGILL

After the acquittal for the Walsh Street murders, Trevor Pettingill lives with his dear old mum in Venus Bay. He has not surfaced too much in the years since and so it would have to be said he has done well. He is not dead and he is not incarcerated, so on the scoreboard he has to be in front. Probably just happy to be home and enjoy some home cooking from mum. When most of the cooks you knew cooked something else, I reckon food would be a real treat.

PETER DAVID McEVOY

Peter David McEvoy moved to Newcastle in New South Wales around 1995 after serving time for an armed robbery. He remained a criminal and has been charged on at least two occasions for assault in NSW. In November 2007, McEvoy was convicted of making phone threats to NSW police after a call he made to them at 1am on 1 February that year. According to press reports McEvoy made comments to police including:

'Police deserve to die and you can get fucked.'

'If I had an M16 I'd wipe out 20 of you cunts.'

'The 12th of October 1988 Steve Tynan and Damien Eyre – what a shame they died. Boo fucking hoo.'

In another incident in February 2005, McEvoy was alleged to have told police who were attempting to arrest him, 'The sweetest thing I ever heard was the police officer's last words while he was dying.'

He was also alleged to say, 'I can't wait to put a shotgun to your head. Loaded up with solid and watching your fucking head get blown up.'

He was sentenced to one-month jail for hindering police and had to serve a further eight months for breaching a bond he was on for breaking someone's collar bone with a baseball bat the year before. He has not repented and moved to NSW as he is a gutless prick who was too scared the very people he says he enjoyed killing would return the favour. He may be dumb, but he isn't completely stupid.

His comments have sparked calls for a retrial since the removal of double jeopardy laws in Victoria in November 2011. The Victorian Parliament passed the Criminal Procedure Amendment (Double Jeopardy and Other Matters) Act 2011 which would allow a new trial to be ordered if there is 'compelling new evidence that a person previously acquitted of a serious crime was in fact guilty'.

In February 2013 press reports carried the story that a new police review conceded there was insufficient new evidence to retry the men accused of the Walsh Street murders. This was yet another blow for the families of Steve Tynan and Damien Eyre who have had to live through numerous rejected applications for a new Coroner's Inquest which could recommend charges if they found who had caused the deaths of the two policemen. This was what I would assume to be the final straw in relation to any new investigations or criminal proceedings against McEvoy. If there is a God, this degenerate son of bitch will meet a grisly end one day and I for one will enjoy a cool soothing ale when he does.

THE GANGLAND WARS

The shooting deaths of numerous crooks in the past decades has seen the demise of so many of the so called 'colourful characters' of the Victorian Criminal Scene. The long list of the dead includes:

Alphonse Gangitano was shot dead in his home in January 1998. No one was ever charged but it was suspected Jason Moran pulled the trigger.

Mark Anthony John Moran. Shot dead outside his Aberfeldie home allegedly by Carl Williams.

Dino Dibra was shot dead in October 2000. It was stated by police on the Purana Taskforce that Andrew Veniamin carried out this shooting.

Victor Peirce was shot dead in Bay Street Port Melbourne by Andrew Veniamin in May 2002.

Nikolai 'Nik' Radev was shot dead in Coburg in April 2003. It was suspected Carl Williams and Andrew Veniamin were behind the murder but were never charged.

Jason Matthew Patrick Moran was gunned down in June 2003 along with Pasquale Barbero when they were watching Moran's kids play football. In February 2007 Carl Williams pleaded guilty to his murder but not to Barbero's.

Graham Kinniburgh was shot dead outside his home in December 2003. Although Carl Williams and Andrew Veniamin were suspected of being involved, they were never charged. In November 2015 Stephen John Asling was charged. He was convicted in March 2017.

Andrew Veniamin was shot dead in a restaurant in Carlton in March 2004 by Mick Gatto, who was acquitted of his murder on the grounds of self-defence.

Lewis Moran was murdered at the bar of The Brunswick Club Hotel in Brunswick in March 2004. Keith Faure, Noel Faure and Evangelos Goussis were all convicted of his murder. The hit was alleged to have been ordered by Tony Mokbel who offered $150,000 for the job. In 2007 Carl Williams was also convicted of commissioning the murder of Jason and Lewis Moran as well as Mark Malia and Michael Marshall.

Lewis Caine was shot dead in 2004. Evangelos Goussis and Keith Faure were convicted of his murder.

Mario Condello was shot dead in his driveway in February 2006. It was believed Rodney Collins carried out the shooting.

THE ARMED ROBBERY SQUAD

The eight Armed Robbery Squad detectives charged with the murder of Graeme Jensen fared very well and their charges were either not proceeded with or were acquitted.

Homicide Detective John Hill committed suicide after being charged and did not get to celebrate with the blokes he was alleged to have tried to cover up for.

In 1999 the Armed Robbery Squad was amalgamated with the Prison Squad and the Special Response Squad into the Armed Offenders Squad. This new entity came under considerable attention and was disbanded in June 2006 after an investigation by the Office of Police Integrity. In the business world I was told to effect change and get things working as they should, management had to change the culture of the people or change the people in the culture. This was obviously another ill-fated attempt at police management, if that ever existed, that ended up with the new people in the new squad allegedly doing the same old conduct of the previous squad. The argument is always going to be that hard crooks need hard policing but not everyone agreed then or now. Personally, I think a harder line with some crooks would be a good thing. These days they think they are the bosses not the coppers.

On 13 September the then Chief Commissioner Christine Nixon called a meeting of the squads' members to announce the squad was over and out. There was a public rally staged by the Police Association led by Paul Mullett to have it reinstated but that was not to be. That was the end of the most controversial squad in the force's history.

Isn't it ironic that during the rally led by Mullett he told the crowd that disbanding the squad would lead to 'what's currently occurring in NSW; drive by shootings, ethnic gangs, race gangs, youth gangs, street gangs, gang rapes by the day'. What a speech. Was he crazy? As if we have gangs running rampant through the streets of Melbourne?

DERMOT AVON

Dermot Avon is an Inspector still in the employ of the Victoria Police. I had cause to speak to him in 2019 as a matter of fact. He has been on the executive of the Victoria Police Association over the years and suffered no obvious ill effects from the charges and subsequent acquittal.

CLIFF LOCKWOOD

Clifton (Cliff) Robert Lockwood went a different path and after being acquitted five years after the shooting of Gary Abdullah he resigned from the force after 12 years. He went into private enterprise running a locksmith business before that failed. He and his then wife headed to Darwin with the intention of joining the police force there. Unfortunately they accepted his wife and not him. He ended up losing his licence and his job as a taxi driver and headed overseas.

He spent time in Dili before returning to the Northern Territory and after an undercover police sting by the NT coppers Cliff was charged with serious drug offences. He failed to appear twice after that and an arrest warrant was issued for his arrest. He ended up handing himself to the Darwin police and lost his bail money.

He was subsequently jailed in the Northern Territory for 15 months as a result of the drug charges he ended up pleading guilty to. But not without having one last crack at putting up some nonsensical defence as to how he came in possession of the 1856 tablets he thought were cold and flu tablets. He apparently offered the undercover cop another 10,000 tablets after the first transaction. As compelling as that argument must have seemed to the magistrate, he went the other way. This time he was not smiling at the end of this appearance and went into the can to serve his time. What he has turned his hand to since his release I don't know nor really care.

JOHN NOONAN

John Noonan left the police force after 40 years' service and remained the rallying point for several attempts to have a Coronial Inquest into the Walsh Street Murders. He has provided immeasurable support to both the Tynan and Eyre families which has lasted through to current times. He was a dogged investigator and finished up as a Detective Inspector. He went on to become the President of Security for the Linfox Group where he stayed for 11 years. He is currently the Global President of Security for the Toll Group.

He is still my brother funny enough and we keep in regular contact. He may have achieved considerably more than me in the corporate world but he still harbours a deep resentment that he was not blessed with my superior comedic skills, devilish good looks and commanding singing voice. These are the crosses he bears and there is absolutely nothing he has been able to do to get close to me in any of the three categories.

DETECTIVE X

When not in hiding from organised crime figures or interstate police due to his amazing investigative skills, he has authored some very successful books based on his endeavours. Even though this may be at odds with a letter allegedly written by his partner from the early years who wrote a rather scathing appraisal of some of his claims after their marriage failed.

I remember his harrowing trip to Malta during the Task Force. The birthday party in the witness protection apartment of Witness X. The superior idea to take the witness to the bush to have her 'serviced'. His later accusation that I hit him outside the Victoria Police Club.

I would call him a modern–day Walter Mitty, while many others in and out of the police force would call him much worse. He must appeal to someone as they keep printing what he writes and even popped him into a miniseries based on his latest investigation in Tasmania, where every time his head appears it has underneath 'Former Homicide Squad Task Force Detective' or similar.

I started watching it but I couldn't stick it out. The overdone facial expressions with the hand on his chin in a pensive moment, the pursing of the lips and the furrowed brow on his important findings. It was too much. He is certainly a crime fighting legend. Ask him.

THE ENSEMBLE CAST

The rest of the crew that were on the Walsh Street Task Force remained in the police force for years and some are still there today.

JIM O'BRIEN

Jim O'Brien went on to head up the Purana Task Force responsible for the investigation of the numerous killings that were the Gangland Wars. He was at the helm when Tony Mokbel was arrested in Greece after fleeing Australia. He left the police force in 2007 and again went to work under my brother at Linfox. After the task force Jim had a medal struck for all the Purana Task Force member to commemorate their achievements.

He also had to endure some hardships within the Victoria Police Crime Department in admitting they had not sworn their search warrants. In an article by Andrew Rule in the Herald Sun in December 2011, the court hearing heard an apology from him to the court and the community for 'inadvertently' adopting what had become accepted practice in the task force.

Attorney general Robert Clark announced on his website on 28 February 2012 that the Victorian Government would introduce legislation to address the problems that arose during numerous court cases where the failure to swear warrants were being used to appeal for evidence to not be allowed. It stated: 'The legislation is not intended to excuse or endorse the failure of some Victoria Police members to follow proper requirements for the making of affidavits. Rather the legislation is intended to prevent the possibility of trials being jeopardised because of possible procedural defects in the swearing or affirming of affidavits... The bill will apply to affidavits made before 12 November 2011 and to any subsequent processes issued or actions taken in reliance on those affidavits.'

That would have been an embarrassing chapter and a sad way to finish such a publicised and celebrated career.

There has been mention he will also have something to say during the public enquiry into the Lawyer X Scandal. Seeing as she allegedly played such a large part in the intelligence gathering during the investigation and then the locating of Mokbel in Greece, he as head of the Purana Task Force would have been involved in some shape or form. But who knows. Time again will tell.

PETER SPENCE

Former Senior Sergeant Peter Spence, or Spencey, was my boss at the Major Crime Squad and great friend until his untimely death in 2017. I was privileged to speak and act as pallbearer at his funeral. I wrote and read an ode written in honour of him.

Victoria Police is saddened, it's lost a keeper of the peace,
He had no fear of falter as he marched into the breach,

He led a team of coppers at the Major Crime Squad Lair
Not all were known as gentlemen, their mantra fear not fair
He stood tall and strong – with a glare that would transfix,
Any miscreant or ne'er do well, or other unlucky--------chap!

The emblem of the majors was the sledgy and shotty crossed
with cuffs,
The modus operandi changed at times, but mostly ended rough,
The Boss was possessed of a voice set deep and eyes to penetrate
The smile reserved for those that passed the sentry at his gate

He loved a beer or 50 and his temper could run hot
A railway station telly felt the calibre of his shot!
He wielded a Remington shotgun or the sledge for the doors,
And the sight of that big man angry, stole their courage for
their cause,

He was the protector of the diamonds at the Melbourne Cup
for years,
They lived in constant fear of theft and Argyle paid in beers,
And Alphonse Gangitano made a threat to our boss one night,
and visit him we did,
He was no fearsome man that morn but a crying bedwet kid,

He was a mate forever loyal and always kept in touch,
He was well respected by all his mates and cherished just
as much,
His beautiful wife Katrina stood by his side until his
peaceful end,
He always knew he'd found his love and closest loving friend,

So care not what the watcher does, as he walks along that wall,
His job was to protect and serve and answer to the call,
Now his smile is softly smiling down on all who were lucky
enough to know
A big strong bloke with a heart of gold, who never feared to go,
He would give his best endeavours and fight in our defence,
Victoria Police has lost a bloody good man, in Senior Sergeant
Peter Spence.
Vale my friend.

I watched another police story from years ago about former
hitman Christopher Dale Flannery and gangland thug Alphonse
Gangitano. There walking along beside Flannery during one of his
many arrests was Peter Spence. There are plenty of stories about
Peter but that is enough for today.

MARK WILEY

Mark and I kept in contact during the years since we both left
the police force. Mark was at the Armed Robbery Squad and was
nearly killed during a raid on the home of one of the Russell Street
bombers Peter Reed. It was a much-publicised shooting on Anzac
Day 1986 when he was shot after Reed fired four shots at him,
hitting him with the last one. He came close to death a couple of
times as a result of that bullet.

We would catch up in Melbourne in the years preceding his
suicide. The weight of the wounding and the battles with PTSD
took their toll over the years. I went to a luncheon with Mark
and Peter Spence at an exclusive club in Melbourne a couple of
years before his death. It was the up-market Savage Club where
Peter was a member. We had a big lunch with many fast beers and
ended with a Sloe gin or two. We talked in depth that day about

what the impact of policing had on him. He was a proud member of the Armed Robbery Squad and yet mentioned his deep-seated resentment at some of the blatant bullshit that some people spoke.

He said while nearly dead in hospital and during his recovery that some members of the Armed Robbery Squad would tell him how lucky he was to have been shot! Seriously. He sat there staring into space at the club recounting one or two of those conversations and his incredulity at anyone thinking let alone saying that. There were plenty of good blokes at the Armed Robbers in those days and like anywhere else there were some cowboys who thought like that.

I spoke to Mark days before he died and we met for coffee only a week or two prior. He was distracted and preoccupied as I have seen others that have suffered PTSD become. He was not in a good place and we spoke of his perceptions of things happening in his life at that time. It was unfortunately no surprise when he took his life. He was a very intelligent man who suffered from demons he could not tame. Rest in peace now.

It is funny I still have Mark's number in my mobile along with Peter Spence. I haven't been able to delete them as there is some weird feeling that would be the finish. I am not ready to do that just yet.

I still keep in touch with a couple of the blokes that go back to the St Kilda days and then Walsh Street. In 2019 I caught up with Bill Panagiotaros who is still in the job in rural Victoria. In a complete coincidence one of my kids ended up at the same station some 30 years after we worked together. Bill was able to fill in some of the details from St Kilda and the task force and it was great to catch up with him again. He still looks the same as he did in the '80s and I can only put that down to his wife of all these years, Helen.

THE POLICE FORCE BECOMES
A DEPARTMENT

Over the years the police force has changed. Some say for the better, most I know say for the worse. The years have seen the coming and going of some rather controversial Chief Commissioners in Christine Nixon, Simon Overland and some alleged shenanigans from several commissioned ranks in recent times. The job has no doubt changed as can be seen by the current uniforms, hair styles, the introduction of gender acceptance, racial equality and even marching in the Gay Pride March. Now that is a far cry from the 1980s and that is to be accepted.

The police force is now operated as a corporate entity with what used to be squads and regions run as independent businesses. Public opinion seems to be the measure of success for the modern world of policing. Again, this is not a bad thing and there has to be continuous learning and education of current leaders in modern management practices, rather than relying solely on rank in a hierarchical structure to get things done. The days of 'yes sir, no sir' have gone. All ranks have a say and a voice and that should lead to greater harmony within the job and a better result for the good people of Victoria.

There have been some monumental problems such as previously mentioned with Christine Nixon ducking out for an elongated bite on the night of the worst natural disaster in the state's history, that was Black Saturday. The debacles with the non-swearing of warrants. The Noel Ashby, Paul Mullett public showdown with the OPI and the demise of all three.

Now we are battling some more current dramas that may make all before it seem inconsequential. The Lawyer X Scandal is of mammoth proportions and the fallout is only just starting to be felt now. This is where a lawyer representing some of the state and country's biggest names in criminal trials was a registered police informer. The latest discovery is that there may have been more lawyers registered as informers without their knowledge.

LAWYER X SCANDAL

The Lawyer X scandal could lead to numerous retrials for people such as Tony Mokbel, who I believe has already begun proceedings to have his cases reviewed. The allegations that Lawyer X had relationships with all sides over many years adds to the scandal and deepens the murky pool that all involved now find themselves wading through. How clean they are when they finally get out will be more than interesting and the changes to the way police manage informers, as well as the oversight requirements on future registrations, will no doubt change significantly. The fundamental belief that the accused has a privileged right to communicate with their lawyer is the foundation stone on which the criminal justice system is build. The erosion of this foundation has the potential to bring the whole house of cards this represents tumbling down around all involved.

IBAC INQUIRY INTO POLICE CONDUCT

An even more recent drama, that is still unfolding, is into the Independent Broad-Based Anti-Corruption Commission, or IBAC investigation, and taking of statements into the deaths of Sergeant Gary Silk and Senior Constable Rodney Miller in 1998.

The hearing is into the conduct of police investigating the murders and whether statements were changed or 'doctored' to include or remove details deemed deleterious to the investigation. In particular two statements taken from Senior Constable Glenn Pullin that were taken two years apart were both displaying the date of the original statement. Former Homicide Detective Charlie Bezzina was questioned as to his signature appearing on both and he said he had 'unwittingly' signed the second one two years later. I might not be the sharpest tool in the shed but I would read anything I signed and thought that was rather basic police procedure. He ended up saying he made no excuses for signing it.

Another point of conjecture was the fact that under questioning he was also asked about the practice of leaving descriptions out of police statements. He said he 'had heard of police excluding descriptions of suspects in witness statements, but he did not condone the practice.' The inquiry heard other police had been told to remove or exclude descriptions of the offender or offenders that Senior Constable Miller said before he died.

The conjecture arises from Pullin's original statement not having the detail that there were two offenders instead of one. The inquiry was also told by other first responders that 'there were two, one on foot.' Charlie Bezzina's response to this was to tell the inquiry he 'was unaware of Senior Constable Miller's last words until recently.'

THE BLACK DOG BITES

I was living in country Victoria on this day and I read that in the newspaper prior to heading off to work what Peter McEvoy had said about Walsh Street. We lived on five acres surrounded by dairy paddocks and could not see another house from our place. I felt a rage like I had never known as I read what he said. I felt a disengagement from the present and set off on my way to work in a trance of incredulity. I could never understand why people did what they did and this latest instalment was what I felt to be a potent mix of rage and even an odd sense of Déjà vu. I couldn't comprehend the ability of something so long ago to come to the fore again some 20 years later.

I made it about 500 metres from the house on a dirt road that was surrounded by farmland. I was going to work as I had done day in and day out for months. There was no need to choose a route as there was only one. I assume I had probably completed the trip unconsciously on several occasions. Everyone has experienced the feeling of arriving somewhere and not really remembering the drive. Now that is distinctly different to driving after a few beers, as would have been the case in the old days.

I pulled over and my mind was blank. I didn't know where I was going or where I was. It was like someone had erased my memory. I looked at the mobile phone on the seat and picked it up and pushed the number for my wife. She answered and I asked if she knew where I was going. She sounded annoyed that I was asking such a question. She quickly replied, 'To work. What are you talking about?' I said, 'Do you know where I am?' She quickly replied, 'I can see you down the road about half a kilometre. What's wrong with you?'

I hung up and turned around and drove back home and she met me out the front of the house. It started a long and convoluted process to seek help from a police force that did not want to help.

I saw a doctor who diagnosed me with depression and put me on medication. He referred me to a psychologist in Kyabram. I continued to work during this time selling cars in Echuca. I contacted the police association when I was first diagnosed. I spoke to a woman I knew who had worked at the squads and was now at the association.

Initially she put me through to the person who was responsible for making preliminary assessments on Post Traumatic Stress claims. He asked me what the drama was. I said I have had some form of breakdown and had been recommended to seek help from the association. He asked me to give some details of what I had experienced. I said, 'I was on the Investigation Team for the Walsh Street murders, I attended the scene of the fatal shooting of Constable Neil Clinch. I attended the scene of the Abdullah Shooting and was shot at twice. Assaulted on more occasions than I could remember and various other dramas.'

He stopped me then and said, 'Don't go into any more detail as you could cause me stress.' I shut up and sat there on the phone wondering if this was real. I asked him what he meant and he reiterated that he could not listen to any details about shootings and the like as it may cause him stress. I could not believe it. I asked him how the bloody hell I was supposed to tell him what was wrong if I could not go into any details. He told me he would get back to me.

I was contacted again by the woman I knew from twenty something years before. She reiterated it was too long ago and there was nothing they could do to help. This filled me with a rage I had not felt for years.

I told her I had never claimed a cracker while I was in the job. I had never asked for anything and was never given anything. I had worked my arse off literally putting my life on the line and paid my association fees the whole time. Now I actually needed some help they couldn't because it was too long ago and they didn't want to bring all that up again.

That was when I was at my lowest. The job I had loved, fought, bled and almost got shot for had abandoned me. Any affinity I had for the Victoria Police Force was vanquished then and there. I could not believe they wouldn't help me. I spoke to my brother and to be honest he thought what I had thought up to that point that PTSD was bullshit, put up by people who didn't want to work or were looking for a payout. He never said that to me, but I felt that was what blokes around my vintage were thinking.

I went to the next appointment with the psychologist and he suggested I lodge a Work Cover claim myself and bugger the Police Force and the Association. So I did. He also told me that the level of trauma I had lived through and with since was beyond his skills and qualifications and that he was going to refer me to a psychiatrist. I was initially taken aback. A psychiatrist. What was going on. Was I crazy?

He referred me to an expert psychiatrist who was a 20-year Airforce Officer who now treated mainly PTSD sufferers from the military services. I travelled to Melbourne to his offices and from the time I met him and did his tests and questionnaires it was obvious this bloke knew what he was talking about.

I remember filling out these questionnaires about PTSD and thinking someone must have got into my head and written the questions from there. They addressed the excessive drinking to sleep or forget, the nightmares, the irrational behaviours specific to PTSD such as anger and depression. He told me I had one of the highest scores he had encountered in his time. I initially thought this was good until he explained it wasn't. It was not a test to do well in. He said if I was ex-military I would have been classified Total & Permanent Injury, commonly referred to as TPI, straight away and would have been treated very differently.

He did my reports and after three months from lodging my Work Cover claim it was eventually accepted. Everyone was very happy that I could now get the treatment I needed and be paid whilst it happened. I had left the car selling due to an altercation with someone that ended with me having to be restrained. I did not return to work and was home up until seeing the psychiatrist.

After speaking with Gallagher Bassett who manage the medical claims on behalf of the Victoria Police Department, I was eagerly awaiting some money. The big days comes and I received a cheque

in the mail. It was for about $180. I thought this must have
been a travelling reimbursement as they said they would pay me
retrospectively for going to appointments.

I called Gallagher Bassett and spoke to my case manager. I asked
what the cheque was for and she replied that was my week's salary
on claim benefit. I sat there again incredulous trying to think
straight through the effects of the tablets I was on to stop me
thinking. I said a 5th or 6th years Detective Senior Constable was on
about $80,000 a year. She replied they had assessed my initial injury
was when I was first shot at by Donald Hatherley in 1983 and that
was the date of injury. She then explained that I was a constable at
that stage and that was the rate of pay I was entitled to.

I said that surely the pay was indexed to inflation and she very
quickly told me they were not compelled to index the rate of pay.
Again, I was dumbfounded. I sat there unable to speak, engulfed
again by a rage that the medication was trying to fight. I could not
believe it. I thought I had won and life was fair again. How stupid
was I. When was life fair? Back to reality.

I went back to work and did my best to perform and stayed on
the medication. I had split up from my wife of 20 years during
all of this. I do not think it was solely due to the PTSD or the
continual fighting with everyone trying to win something I would
probably never win. I spent most of the last year of my marriage
on the couch. I was too scared I would hurt her in my sleep when
I was having one of my far too regular dreams of dead policeman
and fighting everyone.

I remember one night I woke up with my hand around her neck
and was fully intent on punching her face in. I knew it was her and
not whoever I was fighting in my dream and it took all my self-
control not to hit her. She was looking at me terrified and I still
feel terrible about that today. I then slept on the couch to make

sure that would not happen again. We separated not long after when she told me she thought we had drifted apart. I packed up and moved back to Melbourne and into the back of the garage at Mum and Dad's, where I lived as a kid.

I could not pay a mortgage and three kids at school on $180 a week so I took a job back in security and that was the end of the marriage and my reliance on Victoria Police for anything. Thanks for nothing.

I ended up going to court trying to get some level of comfort from Victoria Police for all the physical injuries suffered and the psychological trauma I had endured for over 20 years. I ended up failing as the judge thought as I was now in a new relationship with my now fiancé Susan and that I was in a responsible and well-paying job that I had as a result not suffered any loss or injury to a specific level. I took in three psychiatric reports all stating I had suffered considerable trauma and should not be working.

The courts knew more than these eminent medical professionals and although I was very nicely thanked for my service by the defence counsel I was not sufficiently injured to be at the required level of impairment.

So, I lost the court case and continued on with my litany of disappointments from the police force, the government, their insurers and now add the courts as well. That was it. I vowed never to ask any of them for anything again.

In the end they did me a favour. I had to stay in work and I had to work my way through the PTSD and I continued on for a short time with the psychiatrist and the Victorian Trauma Centre, but ultimately I couldn't afford the time or the expense. I did not want to talk about anything anymore, as to me there was no point. No one really gave a rat's ass, so get on with life and do the best you can.

It ended up working well for other serving as well as former police and military people I have come in contact with all over Australia and beyond. I was able to recognise in them the anger, the violence, the drinking and the general disfunction that is PTSD. I was able to relate to them and advise them to seek the help I had. Many did and most have thanked me for the recommendation. There are a few serving police in Victoria and beyond that are now on full benefits and receiving the treatment they required. So that was some good to come out of not much that was good for me.

I have made it through relatively unscathed. I have battled through and come out the other end. My marriage to Andrea lasted 20 years and we had three fantastic kids who I love dearly.

Two of our children, Sarah and Bryce, are both gainfully employed. Sarah obviously does not listen to her dad. She joined the police force and is still in their employ. Bryce joined the Australian Army and is stationed in South Australia attached to an Infantry Battalion. Sophie is the third and youngest and is at university and is a talented singer. I speak to all the kids daily or close to and am very proud of all of them.

I met and fell madly in love with a gorgeous lady after a year or two on my own after the marriage broke down. Susan is now my fiancé and we live together in suburban Melbourne.

So, life is pretty good really and when you consider what has become of some former colleagues and adversaries, I reckon life is even better than pretty good.

It has been an interesting ride and goes to show you do not have to be a superstar to be involved in some of the biggest stories the police force in Victoria has seen. It has been a pleasure bringing the stories to life for you and if you like this book, there is another one ready to go!

ABOUT THE AUTHOR

Joe Noonan joined the Police Academy in 1981. He progressed through uniform to CIB as the youngest detective that year, passed Detective Training School in 1986 and passed a special sitting of the Sergeants Exams after Walsh Street Task Force. He worked at City West, D24, St Kilda, St Kilda Special Duties, Fitzroy CIB, CIB Major Crime Squad and then seconded to Homicide Task Force for Walsh Street. He resigned after finishing Walsh Street and going back to Major Crime. Joe has also worked in senior management of security and emergency response before moving back into Territory Management for Construction and Heavy Equipment Sales.